THE
AUDITION
BOOK

THE AUDITION BOOK

REVISED AND ENLARGED THIRD EDITION

ED HOOKS

BACK STAGE BOOKS
An imprint of Watson-Guptill Publications/New York

Editor: Amy Handy
Designer: Bob Fillie, Graphiti Design, Inc.
Production Manager: Hector Campbell

This book is dedicated to my daughter, Dagny,
who reacquainted me with *The Little Engine That Could*.

Acknowledgments

Suddenly, you find yourself on stage, and you're happy there are others there with you. My thanks to Bob Bancroft for helping me find my voice, Fred Weiler for not letting me use it too much, Paul Lukas, Janet Rotblatt, Beverly Long, Jim Fox, Mark Locher, Dennis Danziger, Marie Salerno, Jean Schiffman, Marcelo Tubert, and especially Cally.

Contents

Foreword

If one function of the critic is to remind us that we are entitled only to our labor and not necessarily the fruits thereof, it is possible that auditions exist to remind us that we may not even be entitled to the work.

I have been auditioning for thirty-one years so far—from the ages of seven to thirty-eight—and one thing I've learned is that, just like our chroniclers in the press, the business of going after the job is here to stay.

Even when you're no longer auditioning in the most conventional sense—taking your dignity and talent in hand and giving it your best shot in front of strangers—you're still being auditioned. Your last piece of work is being analyzed for its critical/financial success or failure. Your physical qualifications for a role are being considered. People are even asking if you're good to work with or a pain in the neck. And, in these situations, you frequently don't even get the chance to show them what you can do.

Many is the actor who, after years of success and popularity, finds himself not only in the position of being required to go after a role, but feeling with his heart that he *wants* to go after it. That he *must* have it. That he and only he can truly bring it to life. Then, if he lands the job, he feels the exhilaration of knowing he can still hold his own against all comers; that he is, in fact, not only in the profession he loves most, but in the one he deserves to call his own.

This may be the most salutary psychological aspect of the painful, nerve-wracking process of the audition. It serves to remind us of how privileged we are when we get to do what pleases us the most: perform.

As actors, we live much of our professional lives in a posture of supplication: "Please, may I have permission to act?" "Please, may I take another second to prepare for this close-up?" "Please, can we go through this bit again? I don't quite seem to have it yet." But most of all, "Please appreciate me. Please like me." The art we perform is a service, and so we aim to please. Most important, we must please ourselves through the work. But the fact is that if we don't please others as well, we'll eventually get the hook.

The good news is that we're all in the same boat. We're all "on the street" in some measure, and it is this sense of a shared experience that gives the book in your hand its warmth of tone, its qualities of reassurance and unsentimental pragmatism.

Ed Hooks knows whereof he speaks—and he speaks well. His ability to organize our ideas about a process that can, at the wrong moment, turn even the most seasoned professional into a histrionic pudding, allows us to draw a clear bead on the target and helps us all to take those necessary deep breaths.

Yes, it seems unfair. Yes, there are too many people after the same job. Of course, the folks you read for may be not only hopelessly unimaginative but callous as well. And yes, most of the actors who get the jobs you wanted can't hold a candle to your shining talent. Yes, yes, yes! Well, all this and fifty cents will get you a very bitter cup of coffee. You want to get up on the wicked stage? Get in line and sing for your supper.

This book is full of things you should know, and also good advice on what you should do—and there's nothing highfalutin about it. The underlying philosophy, naturally, is use what's best for you and do what you need to do to get the job. But the method of the book—its categorizing and specific nature—keeps it from being a useless, generalized pep talk.

I have only auditioned once for a commercial—when I was about nine or ten years old. It was for a well-known national bus line, and I didn't get the job. The people doing the casting very kindly took my parents aside and told them that, though I seemed to be a nice enough boy with the right qualifications, unless I had the birthmark (their term was "blemish") removed from my left cheek, I probably wouldn't get much work. It was decades later that I finally did make a commercial, but that's another story. The point is, I don't know beans about commercial auditions, and if my parents had listened to those folks, someone with a "blemish" would now be getting all my jobs. The advice Ed Hooks gives about this metier comes from long and fruitful experience, and I learned a great deal from him here.

I know a bit more about auditioning for roles in the theater, television, and film. But the sheer volume of common sense and information in this book gives me pause. Maybe, if I'd known there was so much to deal with, I wouldn't have tried. The answer, of course, is: Put the facts to use! Use your head. God knows, as soon as you hit the ground running and give that reading, you'll be using your heart for all it's worth. Method is essential. Your tank may be filled with the high octane of your talent, but you still have to drive the car. When I read this book, I felt it could help us all to keep our hands on the wheel.

I always look at dramatic auditions as a chance to act. I find that there is much more of an opportunity to use the technique of acting in an audition than we normally assume. In fact acting is, theoretically at least, something we're qualified to do. So if one treats the dramatic audition as a piece of work in itself, one is at least on familiar ground. You may not get the job, but you're focused on the work, the scene, your partner, not just on how you're "doing." I see a lot of acting in theaters (particularly waiver theaters) that looks more like auditioning than the real thing. It's focused solely on the performance (not the technique of getting through the performance) and not really on the role or the text. In fact, it seems to be focused on the actor and his or her Self. Having sat many times on the "safe" side of the audition table, I can tell you that the more involved you are in the business of playing the scene, the more naturally your own qualities as a performer emerge.

All this has to do with fear, and fear, as Eleanora Duse once told a gifted young colleague, is vanity—the vanity of wanting to please, the vanity of fearing to fail. Auditioning can be a fearsome business. So the most important thing is to *do*, to *act*, to *be* what we have told ourselves we are, what we must *know* we are if anyone else is to believe in us. And then, all will be well; and with any luck and talent, we'll land the role.

In the meantime, thank heaven (and Ed Hooks) we have this book, with its humor, its knowledge, its accessibility. It is for all of us at some level, and it's written by a pro, one who not only wants us to get a callback—he wants us to get the job.

I can almost hear Ed Hooks saying, "Congratulations!"

RICHARD THOMAS
Hartford, Connecticut

Introduction to the First Edition

We are auditioning in one way or another for most of our lives, first as children crying for mom's attention, later for that perfect after-school job, then for the favors of a lover; we audition for the limited space in the best colleges and for positions on the good rungs in the corporate ladder; we audition for the basketball team, the cheerleading squad, and, if we go into politics, for votes. Someone even made a bumper sticker out of it: "Life Is A Constant Audition."

You'd think, therefore, that actors would sort of accept auditioning for roles as a matter of course, that the procedure would be something for which life has at least mentally prepared us. Unfortunately, that's not the case. The most sensitive and talented actor may be perfectly lousy in audition, rarely getting the opportunity to work at his or her or craft, and the most mediocre performer may be supremely adept at pushing the buttons of the producers and directors, managing merely to muddle through the performance once hired.

If you want to be a professional actor, you have two major decisions to make: (1) That you are going to be an artist rather than merely a device through which a playwright speaks, and (2) that you are going to be paid. The suffering and broke artist who is living in a cold-water flat is a bad joke. There is no virtue in destitution. You don't become a better person because of it, and you certainly don't become a more talented artist. As an actor, the product you are putting into the marketplace is you and your sensibility, and that has a value that can be measured in monetary terms as well as human ones. The distinction really isn't between those who audition well and those who don't, but rather between those who intend to be paid and those who aren't convinced their skills are worth the money. There is a big difference between auditioning for a role in your church play and a role in the next Neil Simon play on Broadway—money.

In the professional theater, people get paid to do what they did for free in high school. Yet many individuals make the transition from amateur to professional status without really thinking about this fact. They know it, but they don't name it. Suddenly, the stakes are higher, the competition searingly hot, and your confidence is put to the test. If you are doubtful about your place in the professional arena, you will pull your punches in audition, and you won't get cast. In this business, more than in any other I can imagine, self-doubt will sink your boat. If you are not absolutely convinced that you are the best one for the role, that there is a value to be placed on what you are doing, I guarantee they will not cast you. Call it arrogance if you want, but it is the defining characteristic of actors who work.

The accepted wisdom among professional actors is that the real job is the search for work; the actual acting is the fun part. That is why we are always on our way to an audition. Yet to say that we audition a lot doesn't tell the whole story because, contrary to popular belief, auditioning is not a generic activity. Those of us who make our livings at this know well that it would be insanity to try the same techniques at an audition for a stage play that we use for commercials. You don't do the same things when auditioning for an industrial film that you do for a feature film, and, of course, auditions for voice jobs are different from all of the above. This perspective is what led me to write this book. I decided that there is value in a real-world examination of the different kinds of auditions an actor might get in the course of a week. It is my aim to highlight the ways various auditions are similar and to contrast the ways these auditions differ.

My personal background allows me to shine a rather broad light on this subject: twenty-five years in New York and Hollywood, working as an actor, a teacher, and occasionally as a casting director. I've been seen on the New York stage, in regional theaters and stock, in films, and on hit television shows. My on-camera commercials number upwards of 150, many for leading national advertisers, and I've acted in countless corporate/

educational films. And, for fifteen years, I have conducted professional-level workshops in acting and audition technique. Currently, I am bi-city, dividing my time between San Francisco and Los Angeles, frequently heading for the airport.

I've looked at the process from every conceivable angle over a long period of time and in every media; I've been on both sides of the table and have learned that auditioning is a skill that can be mastered. There is much that an actor should be doing if he or she wants to get hired consistently, and there are many pitfalls to avoid. However, the last thing I want to do is lure the unsuspecting innocent into this field. Acting is a devilishly difficult way to make a living and, as the old saw goes, "If there is any way you can avoid doing it, do so." I don't want to suggest that, by reading this book, a novice can breeze right through the glittering gates of stardom, because it just isn't so. However, if the die is cast, or if you are already involved in the pursuit of an acting career and want to improve your averages, I believe this perspective will be useful to you.

This book is divided into three sections. The first two explore the audition process, discuss what the various kinds of auditions have in common and what they don't, and offer step-by-step ways to prepare for each. The third part of the book addresses the unavoidables that must be dealt with in order to get to the auditions in the first place, such as finding an agent, getting good photographs, and joining the unions.

The fact that actors spend such a big chunk of their time in pursuit of work is illustrated by a story I heard Richard Benjamin tell back when he was first coming to prominence as an actor. After reading for the movie *Goodbye Columbus,* he smiled, thanked the people, and turned to leave the room.

"Wait," the director called after him. "You are exactly what we want for the part. We need to talk about your availability."

"Pardon me?" responded Benjamin.

"We want to hire you for the picture."

"Oh, no," said the actor. "You must be making a mistake. I only do auditions."

And so it seems for us all. In fact, I think I hear my agent calling now.

Introduction to the Third Edition

As I was preparing this revised third edition of *The Audition Book*, an interesting statistic came across my desk. At its ratings high point in mid-2000, the hit CBS-TV reality show *Survivor* was seen in 15 million households (out of a possible 100 million). Compare this to *Roots*, the hit television show of the 1970s. At its high point, *Roots* was seen in thirty-six million households (out of a possible seventy-one million). Let me underline that: Fifteen million viewers represents a smash network hit in the year 2000; thirty-six million viewers made a hit in the mid-1970s. Where did all the viewers go? To cable networks and to the Internet, that's where. There are more people watching the tube today than ten or fifteen years ago, but they are spread out across the multimedia landscape. Because there is more programming for viewers to choose from, there are more acting jobs today than there used to be, but they are popping up in new places and on average pay less than did hit network shows of the recent past. The actor who wants to build a career in the twenty-first century, therefore, must develop a new game plan based on a different frame of reference than was used by the preceding generation of actors.

I have added an entirely new chapter to this edition, "The Internet and Digital Filmmaking." This will go a long way toward explaining what is happening in the entertainment industry today and what actors ought to do about it. With this new content, I have attempted to refocus actors who may have purchased earlier editions of this book, and I have generally updated all the other chapters. For example, since the last edition, Screen Actors Guild has merged with the Screen Extras Guild. (SAG execs will tell you that it wasn't really a merger, but they're playing word games. It was a merger.) Industry trade paper *Backstage* merged with Hollywood's *DramaLogue,* forming something called *Backstage West—DramaLogue,* and both of them show up now on the Backstage Internet web site, www.backstage.com. Advertisers are spending $2 billion a year now advertising on the Internet, a medium that wasn't even on the ad-revenue radar screen five years ago.

Some things never change, though. Auditioning is still auditioning, and it is still a stressful activity. Actors still have to take script in hand and do their stuff in audition rooms large and small in pursuit of work. I've left alone those parts of the book that deal with audition technique, because strategies for winning are the same now as they have always been.

I appreciate the success of past editions of *The Audition Book* and hope you enjoy this new one. It has been my pleasure to write it for you. Good luck with your acting career!

ED HOOKS

PART ONE

AUDITIONING BASICS

CHAPTER 1

Audition Anxiety and What to Do About It

Auditioning produces stress 100 percent of the time. It comes with the turf, and any actor who tells you otherwise is lying. No matter how many times you go through it, you never get used to it, never reach the point where you squeal with delight at the prospect of getting to show your stuff one more time. As your career develops, the stakes only get higher, the stress greater.

More bad news: auditioning is here to stay. Despite the coming of the computer age, there is simply no better way to match actors to roles. The process can't be automated and, until you become a bona fide star, you're just going to have to live with it. Even then you may not escape. Legend has it that Marlon Brando had to audition for *The Godfather* because the producers just couldn't imagine him as a Mafia boss, and he certainly had long since established himself as an international star.

And now the sunshine: stress can be managed in such a way that it won't interfere with your auditions. I won't go so far as to suggest that you will be unaware of it, but you can learn to work with it so at least it doesn't ruin your readings. At times you can even use it to your advantage.

THE SYMPTOMS OF AUDITION ANXIETY

We all know the symptoms: cotton mouth, tight throat, clammy hands, and rigor mortis of the lips. You might tremble and twitch a little, perspire profusely, or have muscle spasms in your back. Worst of all is how difficult it is to concentrate. Once you start to become aware of your tension, it tends to be the only thing you can think about. Trying to put it out of your mind is like trying not to think of a black duck. And, of course, tension breeds tension, so the whole thing can really escalate.

A few years ago, I participated in some screen tests for *Half Nelson*, a new TV series being produced at 20th Century-Fox. My job was to commit two scenes to memory and then play both with each of the six finalists for the lead role in the show. We were on one of the sound stages at the studio, and the contenders were kept waiting in motor homes in a nearby parking area. One by one, they were escorted onto the set, introduced to me, and given the basic blocking of the scenes.

These were men who, by anybody's standards, would be considered successful. Perhaps they weren't superstars but they were certainly recognizable from other TV shows, stage appearances, and in one case from a singing career. If you saw them, you would think they already had it made. Therefore, I was surprised to watch every single one of them struggle with tension. It was understandable that a new actor in town might be nervous in that situation, but these guys had been around. Still, it took hours to get through the tests because of botched takes, false starts, and too-sweaty faces.

What was going on? Why weren't they confident? Because—now think about this—if you get your own TV series, it is a career turning point, a shortcut to a Beverly Hills address and financial independence. All the performers knew this, knew they were being scrutinized by network executives, producers, and agents, knew that this might be the best shot they would ever get. So the tension on the set could be cut with a knife.

P.S. When it was all over, who do you think got the part? In true Hollywood fashion, it wasn't even one of the nervous contenders. The role went to Joe Pesci, whose movie career was in a momentary dip. I don't think he auditioned, but I can't be sure. Anyway, the series went on the air, lasted six episodes, and is part of TV history. Next case.

It is a well-documented fact that fear number one for *all* people, whether they are actors or not, is having to get up in front of a group and make a speech. There is something inherently unnerving in the transaction. What are they thinking? Am I making sense? Do I look like a nervous wreck? Why aren't they smiling? Where's the exit?

Actors have it even worse, because not only do we have to get up in front of a group and do something, but the specific purpose that got the group together in the first place is to carefully scrutinize our delivery and style. It is very easy to take the position that you are being tested personally, and as soon as you do that, you're dead.

Audition anxiety is a sister of stage fright, and its causes are wrapped up in an actor's personal context as well as the importance of the project at hand. If you are feeling good about yourself in general, you will approach everything you do, including auditions, with more confidence than if you are feeling vulnerable or depressed. If there is a new love in your life, you will carry the euphoria right into the audition room with you; if you have had a string of acting jobs, you're bound to approach this one with confidence. On the other hand, if you haven't worked in six months, that anxiety can cause you to be off-balance, throwing off your timing.

All animals, including human ones, are designed either to fight the thing that threatens them or to run from it. But actors in auditions can do neither. They must stand there with their feet in the fire and try to remain vulnerable to the text. They can't very well pick up a chair and throw it at the producer, and if they run screaming from the room, they surely won't get cast.

At least part of the answer lies in changing the way we view the threat. Think about this: suppose everyone in the audition room was a close friend or relative. Would you still be nervous? Suppose the audition was taking place in your living room at home. Would you still be nervous? Suppose everyone in the audition room except you was eight years old. Would you still be nervous? Why not? What's the variable? You guessed it. In a real professional-level audition, we are dealing with all unknown factors. We don't know the people who are watching our audition; we don't know whether we are on target with our work; we don't know for certain what they are thinking when they watch us; we don't know if we are up against Robert De Niro or Meryl Streep for the role. In short, we are on their turf, doing things on their terms.

But is there really a threat in the audition process? From having sat on both sides of the table, I am certain that most of the danger is a figment of the actor's extremely vivid imagination. The people watching truly want you to do well, want you to get the role. They take no pleasure in seeing you suffer and, if there was something they could think of to ease the tension, they'd do it. Most of the time, they are as uncomfortable about the process as the actors are.

SELF-FULFILLING PROPHECY

All actors need to go back and reread Dale Carnegie's book *How to Win Friends and Influence People*. What a smart man he was! He had a grasp on the concept of self-fulfilling prophecy before there was even a name for it.

In a nutshell, self-fulfilling prophecy means that you will tend to succeed if you think you will succeed, and you will tend to fail if you think you will fail. The proposition has been stated and restated in countless forms: "When you're hot, you're hot," "Money seeks money," "Them what's got, gets," "on a roll," and so on. The point is that success breeds success, and this is never truer than in the audition room.

Put yourself in the position of the auditors. They have built this incredibly expensive race car, and they are looking for someone to drive it. They don't want to hire a person who comes in and fumbles around apologetically while hunting for the ignition. They don't care if you have never driven their race car before, but they definitely want someone who knows how to drive—and likes to do it. What they want is a winner, and a winner is someone who is already winning, not someone who plans to start winning next week.

"But, I'm new at this!" I can hear you protest. "How can I be expected to behave like a winner if I've never done this before?" Well, it comes down to the way you view the problem. Is the glass on the table half-full or half-empty? What is your personal policy in life? Do you normally expect to succeed at what you do? If so, why should an audition room be different? Before you go into the audition room, you know all of the requirements, right? You may have taken some classes in audition technique, and you probably have been through at least a few cold reading situations. Trust that knowledge. Let it give you strength.

Think for a minute about the dynamic of successful working actors. They're not going to be overly concerned with what the auditors want to see; instead, they will show how the role will be played if they are chosen. It's basic.

In my desk at home, I have a study done by a psychologist at Carnegie Mellon University in Pittsburgh. In it, he measured the practical impact of an optimistic versus a pessimistic attitude. First, he invented a standardized test that would categorize individuals as optimistic or pessimistic. Then he began applying variables to each group to measure how they reacted to life's little failures. He tested reactions to such things as being late for an appointment or not getting a date with a desired person. What he discovered was that the individual with an optimistic attitude would invariably attribute failure to circumstances outside his or her immediate control and would plunge back in to try again; the pessimistic person saw failure as sign of his or her own short-comings and inadequacies, the realities of life, and would tend to withdraw.

Then—and this is the fascinating part—the psychologist administered this same test to a bunch of insurance salesmen, people who face rejection every working day. The results were stunning and have major implications for actors. The optimistic group of salesmen sold 37 percent more insurance in their first two years on the job than their pessimistic counterparts! And, what is more, the pessimists were twice as likely to quit in their first year of employment.

A winning attitude is simply essential for actors in auditions. I'm not suggesting that you have to leap into the room grinning and glad-handing everybody, but if you don't think you ought to get the job, they won't either. At the professional level of acting, it is like going out every time and playing Pete Sampras or Steffi Graf. Everybody is wonderful, and a few are downright brilliant. Winning the game—getting cast—can come down to nothing more than who most expects to win.

Some folks say that auditions are won or lost within five seconds of when the actor enters the audition room, and I think there is something to that. How long does it take you to form an impression of the people you pass on the street? It's almost instantaneous. It may not be fair, but it's the way we are wired. First impressions are frequently the most important ones. If you walk into the audition room in your self-protective, uncertain mode, the auditors will feel some doubt about your abilities. They might well decide you are not right for the job before you even open your mouth. And, as anybody who has ever studied plain old Aristotelian logic knows, it is impossible to prove a negative. Once they conclude that you aren't right for the job, it is an uphill battle to prove them wrong about that.

Keith Johnstone wrote a marvelous book entitled *Impro: Improvisation and the Theatre* (Theatre Arts Books, 1989), in which he approaches improvisation from the standpoint of status transactions. As he correctly points out, we are continually negotiating status in life whether we are conscious of it or not. When a teacher steps to the front of the classroom, the students are allowing him or her a position of temporary high status; when you perform a scene in front of your acting class, you are being granted the high status position. Similarly, there is a clear status transaction at play in all auditions. Auditors want actors to take the high status, to lead, to show what they intend to do with the role if they are cast. Actors who are intimidated by the people for whom they are auditioning are not going to be able to lead. Their attitude will be too deferential, too low status.

Again, put yourself in the position of the auditors. How would you respond if an actor meekly entered the room and tried really, really hard not to make any mistakes in the audition? Would you be impressed? Would you want that person to drive your half-million-dollar race car? No, of course not. Remember this; write it on your bathroom mirror: *The avoidance of failure is not the same thing as the pursuit of success.* When you go into an audition, step out boldly, give them something to choose. Don't worry that you will make mistakes that will cost you the job. I mean, you already don't have the job, right? You might as well try something because, in reality, you have nothing to lose.

SOME PRACTICAL EXERCISES

Stress in auditions is undoubtedly caused by mental attitude more than anything else, and the best remedy is going to be mental. You need to learn that you cannot relax by ordering yourself to do so. There is no gain in saying to yourself, "I must not be nervous!" because it will just have the opposite effect. Take a lesson from Masters and Johnson and their studies on male impotence. If a man is nervous and can't perform sexually, the way to solve the problem is to shift his thinking to something positive, namely the pleasure at hand. If he dwells on his nervousness, he'll *never* perform!

Even if you don't feel like it, and you probably won't, go ahead and smile. Make yourself. Go into the bathroom and laugh at your silly self in the mirror. Laughter relaxes you immediately.

Don't just sit there in the chair in the waiting room and fret. Physicalize. Go out in the hallway or outside the building and do something physical. Make some noise. Do jumping jacks, breathe in some deep breaths. Nervous actors are always forgetting to breathe. And don't worry that a producer or director or someone will see you jumping around in the hall. They already think actors are about a quart low anyway.

Try some tongue twisters. My favorite is this combo: "The Swiss wrist watch sank swiftly." and "Peter Piper picked a peck of pickled peppers." Try saying them back to back. Gently slap your cheeks, pucker your lips, force the blood back into your lips. When you are tense, circulation to the extremities drops. This is why your hands are cold. By doing this exercise, you are kind of jump-starting your body. The principle is that, if you can force circulation into your lips, it will help the rest of you relax.

Rehearse success. Boy, is this important, and it is directly related to self-fulfilling prophecy. I do it while en route to auditions. Imagine that you are a fly on the wall at the upcoming audition, and watch yourself go through the entire process as a winner. Watch as you enter the audition room, smiling and full of confidence. See how warmly the auditors respond to you? See how interested you are in them? Watch them relax with you as they realize that you are comfortable with this race car. When the director or casting director gives you some adjustments, watch yourself accept them good naturedly. After the audition is completed, watch yourself leave the room as the auditors smile. Feel the warmth of goodwill and approval.

Picture the auditors sitting there naked. I'm including this little gem because I've heard it about a hundred times. I'm not sure it works, but the idea is cute, and it might get you to smile.

CHAPTER 2

Audition Guidelines

There is a lot of confusion out there about playing a character, and I attribute it primarily to misinformation about the craft of acting. Every time I read an interview with some hot property who explains how he "becomes the character," I cringe because I know another five thousand aspiring actors just got the wrong idea.

I get people in my classes all of the time who think that acting is about "becoming a character," and they keep waiting for some kind of out-of-body experience. "When I'm a character," goes the logic, "I'm not myself." So, in order to construct a character, the first thing they want to do is layer on an accent or a trick voice or something. Of course, what they wind up with is closer to a caricature than a character.

PLAYING A CHARACTER

The truth is that it takes time to develop an intelligent characterization—days, weeks, maybe even months. It isn't something you pull out of a hat at an audition. It involves a close study of the role and hopefully includes a rehearsal process in which you try different approaches, attempting to find the parts of yourself that might have evolved like the character you are going to play. Acting is not about hiding behind a character; it is about exposing yourself through one. When you are doing it well, it feels dangerous, not safe, like walking a high wire without a net.

The best way to approach an audition is to take a long, cool look at what the scripted character is saying and doing in the scenes you will be reading—and accept whatever is going on there as *your* behavior. Don't waste time denying that you would behave or speak the way the character does. Immediately embrace it, and then get busy trying to justify it. The mistake occurs when actors say, "Let's see. I, of course, would never behave like this. What kind of character would behave in this silly fashion? Hmmmmm . . ." Immediately, they're in trouble because they've locked themselves into the impossible task of assembling something purely from external factors.

"But, I would never, not in a million years, talk and behave like the person in this script!" you complain. Oh, yes you would, and yes you will, just as soon as you get into the audition room. Those very words are going to come right out of your mouth, so you might as well motivate them. There is no gain in denial. We are all human, and we are capable of all behavior.

At least part of the confusion comes from the cavalier way the term "character" is bandied about in commercials. I have heard very knowledgeable people advise new actors that they should have "two or three stock characters" for use at commercial auditions. And it is common to hear a casting director ask for "a really fun character." (In some commercials, you get to play nonhuman characters such as a dancing sock or a pickle or a grape, and the ad agency will even send cartoon renderings of the cuddly creatures to the audition.)

The problem is that people who work in advertising are not really part of the entertainment world at all and they understand very little about an actor's craft. Their job is to sell products, period. Like most nonactors, they perceive that an actor "becomes a character," stepping outside of himself or herself and changing into someone or something else. They don't know how we do what we do, only that we do it, and when they ask us for a character at an audition, they think that's a constructive direction. A new actor, one who doesn't have much training, will hear that kind of direction and try to do it rather than translating it into something that is playable.

I once saw a casting director in a commercial workshop reduce a young actor practically to tears by insisting that he render a particular piece of copy as a "Bob Newhart character." The poor guy tried, and she would just shake her head, interrupting him with "No, that's not it. Try again." Finally, she sighed deeply and said, "Well, I guess you just can't do it." Totally depressed, now convinced that maybe he wasn't cut out to be an actor, he took his seat. After class, I sought him out and explained that the fault was not his, that it is impossible to render a Bob Newhart character. You can't be Bob Newhart. You can impersonate him maybe, but that's not what the casting director was after. The actor was in a lose-lose situation because the casting director was unable to enunciate what she really wanted. The only thing he could have done in the face of direction like that was perhaps to try to motivate a befuddled reading because Newhart sometimes comes off that way. It might have satisfied her, but I doubt it.

Creating character voices for cartoons or radio commercials is another matter entirely because you are not being seen. The key is that you are creating illusion, the sound of a character, not trying to portray one on stage, and that is a different craft. Indeed, performers in this field frequently do have a stable of stock "characters," but if you watch them in the recording studio you know in an instant that the process should not be confused with what actors do in developing a characterization in other media.

Am I suggesting that every role you read for be reduced to a rendering of you and your everyday personality? Of course not. I'm only saying that it is a mistake to approach any scripted character with the attitude that you must step outside of your own skin in order to step into that one. You have to find a way to express the character through yourself truthfully. Acting is not about hiding.

One last note on this subject, this regarding the use of accents in auditions. The best policy is to use them only if absolutely necessary. If you are up for the part of an English barrister or a Jamaican singer, by all means try an accent. Otherwise, stick with standard American speech. And whatever you do, don't confuse an accent with "character."

COSTUMING FOR AUDITIONS

There is an open debate among actors regarding the wisdom of extreme costuming for an audition. If you are up for the role of a bag lady, should you wear something from Goodwill and bring the shopping cart?

Personally, I draw the line at really extreme costuming. I got my baptism in New York, where actors have to get around on the subways, and it is impractical to lug costume changes. What you are wearing when you leave your apartment in the morning is what you will wear all day. In Hollywood, on the other hand, actors can toss their entire wardrobe in the trunk of the car, and many do.

One of my closest friends is a big devotee of costuming, and he recently went to an audition at Universal dressed up like Carmen Miranda, complete with high heels and lavish eye makeup. (I love to think of how far he would have gotten on the New York subways.) He didn't get the part, but I'm not going to argue with him about his dress. People who go in for this extreme stuff swear by it. They claim it helps them make a commitment to the role, and it lets the producers see exactly what they are going to get without having to use a lot of imagination. Pick your poison.

This is not to say that you can't wear shorts to a tennis player audition or a swimsuit if they ask for one. No, I'm talking about dressing up like a Dickens character or an infantryman. The best policy in my book is a kind of safe, middle-ground, flexible clothing.

Swimsuit auditions, by the way, are a special kind of trauma, and if you think there is any chance at all you might get one, by all means invest in something flattering. The usual procedure is to wear the swimsuit under your street clothes when you go to the audition. There is less leering than you might imagine; it sort of takes the mystery out of things to have fifty imperfect bodies parading around under strong lights.

YOUR PHYSICAL APPEARANCE

With hair, moderation and flexibility are the keys. It is entirely possible to have an audition for a commercial in the morning and another audition for a period drama in the afternoon. You want to have a hair length and style that will cover both possibilities. Medium-length hair is best for adult men and women, but young girls and teens can get away with long hair. However you cut it, make sure it doesn't fall in your face when you move around. If they can't see your face, they won't cast you.

Hair color is a personal matter, and the only advice I have to offer is to make sure it looks authentic if you elect to color it. Also, if you are gray before your time, you might want to get rid of the gray. When agents and casting directors see gray hair, they immediately put you into an older category. I've talked to many actors in their mid-fifties who were frustrated because they are continually stuck in grandma or grandpa casting calls, competing with actors in their sixties or seventies. The reason? Gray hair. The solution? Dye it.

A note to men regarding mustaches: if you are wearing one because you think it makes you look older, odds are that you should shave it. If you have one of the Clark Gable/Tom Selleck variety, it might be okay. Also, mustaches seem to be more acceptable on African-American than Caucasian men. Generally speaking, facial hair in commercials is a no-no, but it isn't as much of a restriction on TV shows, in movies, or on stage.

If you wear a hair piece, for God's sake get a good one. Don't scrimp. If someone can tell by looking at you that you are wearing a piece, it is a bad piece. And remember, no one is going to volunteer that judgment. You have to be objective about yourself.

Makeup for women is a touchy subject. I see plenty of awful makeup in my classes, and I usually advise a couple of hours with a professional makeup consultant. It could be well worth the money. What looks swell when walking around the shopping mall in Boise might not fly at all in New York or Hollywood. There is a science to applying makeup effectively.

Teenage girls who have been through the modeling schools need to be particularly careful. The schools may be excellent, and they may teach you how to put on makeup, but too many teenagers use makeup to try to propel themselves into an older casting category. If you are in your teens, your money is almost surely in roles that call for the fresh and youthful look, and less makeup is better than more. If you are wearing so much that it is readily noticeable, it's probably too much.

If you need eyeglasses to see, wear them. If you don't like the way they look on you, get contacts. Few things annoy casting directors more than having to watch actors squinting at a script or a cue card because they are too vain to wear glasses. I wear reading glasses when I audition with script in hand, and it hasn't hurt me any. They figure you will not need the glasses once you get to the set and have the script memorized. You might even want to invest in a couple of pairs of "prop" glasses, made with plain glass, preferably the nonglare type. An attractive pair of glasses can throw you immediately into a more businesslike or studious type range. And, of course, never, ever wear darkly tinted glasses to an audition unless they are asked for—especially the glasses that gradually darken the longer they are in bright light. The artificial lights in a casting studio do a pretty good approximation of the sun, and your eyes will slowly disappear from view.

Regarding your weight, a double standard exists in the world of commercials. Men gain weight, and they just become cute "character" types with their pot bellies hanging out; women gain weight, and they are considered fat. It is not fair, but there it is. You can be slim, or you can be a fat character type, à la Roseanne, but you should avoid the middle ground. If you are twenty pounds overweight, for example, you need to lose or gain. A chubby grandma may be okay, but an overweight female account exec or housewife is not. That chunky look can cost you work, no question about it. For my money, the best bet is to let your health dictate your weight anyway. Americans are woefully overweight in general, but commercials do not reflect this. "If I buy this product, I will be like the actor in the commercial," goes the logic. And nobody wants to be fat, least of all women.

AN AUDITION CHECKLIST

Things to do prior to the audition:

- Get a good night's sleep.
- Do not drink alcohol prior to an audition, not even a glass of wine. It might dull your response time.
- Don't drink too much coffee prior to an audition. It might make you feel wired and hyper. You'll be tense enough without extra stimulants.
- Use extra-strong antiperspirants. Nervous tension creates all sorts of body odors.
- Ask your agent if this is a prescreen meeting with a casting director, or if you will be reading directly for the decision makers.
- Ask your agent who the director and the producer are. In the case of commercials, the agent will most often not have this info, but should have it for film, TV, or stage. It's good to know if you are going to be reading for a director who just won awards at the Cannes Film Festival or a producer who already has a hit show on the air.
- Ask your agent if the script is available in advance. (Scripts are never available in advance for commercials, but they frequently are for film, TV, and stage.)
- Ask if there is any particular dress requirement. (Be sure not to wear clothes that show perspiration stains too easily.)
- Ask if there are any parking instructions. If the audition is

being held on a studio lot, will you be provided with a drive-on pass?

- Ask your agent for directions to the audition if you are not exactly sure where it is. You don't want to be late.

Take these items with you to the audition:

- Your photo and resume, neatly stapled together. Do this even if you have reason to believe the casting director already has your photo.
- A highlighter so you can mark your lines on the script.
- Breath freshener. Nervous tension can create bad breath.
- Toothbrush, dental floss. (You don't want to be acting your heart out with a piece of celery stuck between your front teeth.)
- Comb and/or hairbrush. Also take something to pin your hair back if you need to.
- Change for parking meters.

Pointers for the audition itself:

- Don't waste time socializing with actors in the waiting room. Use your time profitably, studying the script, doing some stress-reduction exercises. Think like a champion athlete getting ready for a big game. Stay loose, but remain alert, clear-headed, ready for anything that happens.
- It is a good idea always to be ready with a chatty story of some kind, an ice-breaker. I'm not talking about a monologue, just a subject that interests you that might involve a casting director or producer if the situation should arise. Some people, particularly those in the movie world, may purposely draw you into casual conversation to see your "real" personality, and sometimes these situations just happen by chance. I recall a time when preparation in this area really came in handy. I was auditioning for a Neil Simon movie, and Mr. Simon was in the room. While the director was looking at my resume, Mr. Simon asked me what I had been up to lately, and I mentioned a recent fishing trip. To my surprise, he likes fishing! So, before the reading even started, I had the chance to schmooze with Neil Simon for a few minutes. Couldn't hurt.
- I can't recommend this enough times: Don't worry so much about what you think they are looking for. Show them how the role will be played if they cast you. Put your stamp on it.

After you have completed the audition:

- As soon as you get out of the building, and while these things are fresh in your mind, jot down for future reference the names of the people who saw your audition, and their job function. You never know when you might encounter them in the future. When you get home, transfer this information to your master files.
- Send a thank-you note to the casting director.

CHAPTER 3

Casting Directors

Casting directors work for producers. Some of them freelance and are available to any producer who wants to hire them, and others have full-time staff positions with ad agencies, television networks, movie studios, or production houses. Some operate out of their own plush offices, others out of their apartments; some specialize in casting movies or stage, others in commercials or TV shows; some are men and some are women. Whatever their personal situation, their function is always the same: the casting director's primary job is to go out into the world and find actors to audition for the director and producers. Once the director and producers have decided which actors they want to hire, the casting director is the one who negotiates money, schedules, and billing with the actors and/or their agents. The title of casting director is therefore something of a misnomer because they don't usually have the final say in who gets cast. They mainly determine which actors are going to be seen in audition, and then the bosses make the ultimate choices.

HOW CASTING DIRECTORS WORK

As far as producers are concerned, casting directors can find actors wherever and however they please, but the most common way by far is through franchised talent agents. In a city like Los Angeles, there are something like two hundred agents who are continually pursuing the casting directors, trying to get their clients in on the auditions. The numbers may be smaller in Detroit, San Francisco, or Dallas, but the procedures are exactly the same. Casting directors usually talk to agents when they want actors.

To new actors, casting directors can be a great frustration because it might be hard to meet them; to actors who have been around the track a couple of times, the complaint is that casting directors see them in too narrow a type range. To the talent agent, a casting director may be Mr. or Ms. Wonderful or a pain in the rear but, if you want to get your clients in to see him or her, you have to make nice. To producers, a casting director is the only thing protecting them from that tidal wave of actors out there.

At its finest, casting is more of an art than a craft. An intuitive, insightful, empathetic casting director is worth more than his or her weight in gold to both the producers and the actors. At its most mundane, it is little more than a traffic-cop function and demands respect from few. Casting directors have no union, and there is no school that teaches the skill. The Casting Society of America, based in Hollywood, is a nationwide professional organization of casting directors, but it is not a union in the same sense as, say, Screen Actors Guild. Mainly it is an association through which experienced casting directors can maintain communication with one another. Most casting directors are independent contractors and learn their trade through an informal apprenticeship. Their backgrounds are as varied as the listings in the Yellow Pages. I've seen secretaries, flight attendants, photographers, industry wives, and talent agents become casting directors, but I suspect the most common denominator is that many were aspiring actors at one time. More than a few have stuck a toe in the water to see about acting, jerked it out immediately, and instead gone into casting.

The relationship between actors and casting directors is fascinating because, no matter how much personal chemistry there might be, actors can never get it out of their heads that this is a person who can broker a job, and casting directors can never forget that they are dealing with an actor who badly wants to work. Most of the time, everybody deals with one another in a professional manner, and that is what you should expect if you are a newcomer. Tales of "casting couches" and such are overblown. As in any business, however, standards can break down from time to time, and when they do the result can be embarrassment, awkwardness, or outright injury. I really don't think it is necessary for new people to wear a suit of armor when approaching casting directors, but if you find yourself in a situation that feels uncomfortable, move carefully. You absolutely, positively do not have to compromise yourself in any way to further your acting career, especially sexually or financially.

At an audition, the casting director is the actor's ally. He or she wants you to do a good job, wants you to get cast. If you look good, the casting director looks good. Remember, he or she is bringing you into the audition room to meet the boss, the producer. Therefore, pay close attention to little signals, helpful hints the casting director might give you while escorting you into a reading. I can't count the jobs I have gotten because the casting director whispered in my ear that "they're looking for something really low key and natural" or "they don't know what they want, so be bold." Though he or she may work for the producer, the casting director is your friend.

PRESCREEN INTERVIEWS WITH CASTING DIRECTORS

If a casting director doesn't already know your work, it is understandable that he or she would want to prescreen you before taking you to the director and producers. The way in which this is done varies a bit from medium to medium, however, so we have to look at each one separately.

Commercial prescreens rarely involve a sit-down chat because commercial auditions are typically videotaped. The casting director has the opportunity to get to know an actor during this first taping and has the option of erasing him or her from the tape before forwarding it to the ad agency.

TV and movie prescreens involve a private conversation and a cold reading from "sides" (selected pages from a script). Casting directors will look at your photo and resume and then ask you to read. If they like the reading, they'll go ahead and schedule a time for you to come back and audition for the producers and director. If you are already an actor with some strong credits, a prescreen interview will probably only involve "taking a meeting." Until you get to that point, bring your reading glasses.

Stage prescreens usually include a private chat and an opportunity for you to present a couple of prepared monologues. For more about how to select and present monologue material, see Chapter 9, "Auditioning for the Stage."

The biggest problem with prescreen interviews is that they are frequently sandwiched into a casting director's busy day. Everybody is in a hurry. The telephone may be ringing, people may be going in and out of the casting director's office, and he or she may be distracted. Don't lose your cool if this happens. Hopefully, the casting director will ask for privacy while meeting you but, if not, keep a sense of humor and go with the flow. If the casting director seems distracted during the actual reading, wait for him or her. The actor always has the power to set the pace in a scene. If "sides" are given to you cold, ask for a few minutes to look at them. Don't try to impress the casting director with what a quick study you are. Return to the outer office and analyze the script, mark it up if you want to. You need to have the advantage if you can gain it. Also, if you can incorporate what is going on in the office into your reading, do so. I once had a situation where I was reading a scene that called for a furious outburst. Just as I was getting to the outburst part, the phone started. Clearly, the casting director didn't want to interrupt my reading, so she just let the thing ring and ring. Finally, I stopped, looked right at her, and through clenched teeth—and in character—ordered her to answer the phone, just as if it were part of the scene. She smiled, took the call while I sat there, and when she hung up we picked up the scene right where we left off, using the interruption to further fuel the anger necessary for the scene. It worked: I wound up returning to read for the director and got the job.

INTERNET CASTING

Industry trade papers are peppered with ads for Internet casting companies. These businesses make money by charging actors a fee to be included in an online database of photos and resumes. I will have much to say about them in Chapter 14, "The Internet and Digital Filmmaking." For now, just keep in mind that regardless of where it is done, the procedures for casting are pretty uniform. A casting director who is looking for actors is most likely to contact talent agents because agents have a financial incentive—commissions—to represent the best available talent in the marketplace. The agents submit their actor-clients, audition times are agreed upon, and the auditions take place. The Internet has not changed this basic fact of life—not yet anyway.

PART TWO

AUDITIONING

CHAPTER 4

Auditioning for TV Commercials

Commercials are where the money is. Each year, American companies spend $35 billion (that's billion with a "b") on them. It makes sense when you consider the size of the viewing audience. The average prime-time sitcom will be seen by 10–15 million people, and the Super Bowl, which is usually the highest rated show of the year, attracts 127 million viewers all at one time. The scope is staggering to consider, which explains why commercials are literally the heartbeat of the American consumer-based economy. Members of the Screen Actors Guild earn upward of $700 million annually from this source, accounting for 40 percent of total SAG income! In fact, many SAG members consider themselves to be "commercial actors" instead of simply "actors" and evidently have little interest in appearing in anything else.

You don't need a Ph.D. to understand what is going on in commercials, and you don't have to be a graduate of the Royal Academy to act in them. That's why every Aunt Hilda and her niece wants to do them. When I am traveling around the country and people discover that I teach audition technique for commercials, I invariably find hopefuls lining up for an honest appraisal. "People tell me I have a good face for commercials," they will explain. "Do you think I ought to try it?" It's amazing, really. Sober, responsible adults who wouldn't dream of getting up on the stage and acting in a play are ready to drop everything for the chance to be in a Pampers spot. I've had doctors, lawyers, dentists, psychologists, and even the Ambassador to Nepal in my commercial workshops.

Let's settle it right off, then. Can a nonactor, a regular housewife or a retired cop, make it in commercials? Yep. Is it easy to do it? Not by a long shot. Commercials are not something you pursue on a lark. They require an investment of time, money, and persistence, and the average performer only lands one commercial out of every forty auditions or so. A nonactor who wants to do commercials should reread the first paragraph of this chapter and really reflect on how much money SAG members earn from commercials. Those people are highly motivated, and they are your competition. When you go to auditions, they will be sitting next to you, and it can be unnerving to realize the determination of the average professional actor.

The bright side for the nonactor is that commercials are getting shorter and are using less dialogue. Probably half of all spots on TV now are only thirty seconds long, and the trend is bound to continue. When I did my first commercial (for Holiday Inns) in 1970, almost all spots were sixty seconds long with wall-to-wall dialogue. As ad costs have risen, spots have gotten shorter and are relying much more on mood music and quick-cut editing. In other words, if there is anything that professional actors have over nonprofessionals, it is the ability to use dialogue effectively, and there just isn't as much demand for that skill today as there used to be. It equalizes things a bit.

LIFE AS PORTRAYED IN COMMERCIALS

Consumer Reports magazine once did a study of commercials and discovered that only one in eighteen conveyed any useful information at all. The point of most spots is to reinforce the name of the product in a positive way, to make the viewer feel good about it. That's why they convey the sense of life that they do. As I mentioned earlier, there is an implied visual message in commercials: "If I use the product, I'll be like the person in the commercial." In other words, I'll be happy, have cute kids, a good sex life, no zits.

Can you imagine an entire town populated by the people you see in commercials? No serial killers there, eh? You also won't find overcrowded classrooms, burn centers, corrupt politicians, or dogs with no homes. It's an idyllic world, one in which everyone is happy, healthy (or at least jolly), doesn't need to be too concerned about world events, and is eager to get up in the morning to get at that bowl of cereal. Also, perhaps most significantly, no one reads a lot of books. Let's take a closer look.

The Commercial Woman:
- Likes to do housework. A dirty wall is just another opportunity.
- Likes to trade little household secrets with girlfriends.
- Spends a lot of time shopping.
- Takes care of house and home even if she is holding down a full-time job. She's a kind of good-natured superwoman.
- Never gets depressed or sees a shrink.
- Always has enough energy left at the end of the day to light those romantic candles.

The Commercial Man:
- Brings home the bacon.
- Knows next to nothing about household products. Send him to the store for a cleanser, and he will invariably bring home the less expensive Brand X.
- Always makes enough money to afford a house with a nice big yard, usually big enough for a sit-down-type mower.
- Only displays intelligence when it comes to buying cars, insurance, camping equipment, beer, or computers.
- Is an avid sports fan.

The Commercial Kid:
- Is always cute, scruffy, and precocious.

Because commercials portray such an innocent, conservative sense of life, and because women—even professional ones—are usually depicted as homemakers, sophisticated actresses can sometimes be offended by them. Women's rights have been the subject of long, difficult battles in America, and it can be frustrating to turn on your TV and see commercials in which women seem to be primarily interested in the search for a better mayonnaise.

I mention this because I have encountered the problem so many times in my classes, and it is critical that it be overcome. If the ad agency executives suspect that you are harboring resentment about the way a woman is portrayed in a spot, they will pass on you. They really want to cast actors who are "team players," people who are wholeheartedly joining in the sales effort. And, even though women now officially bring home half of the income in American families, the fantasy persists that men are the main bread winners, and women take care of the home. Commercials reflect this fantasy much more than being a mirror of how society really is.

If this is a problem for you, try looking at it this way: A commercial is an acting job, right? It is just the same as if you were acting in a TV show or a movie. Acting is acting. If you were hired to portray a commercial star in the next Julia Roberts movie, could you do it honestly? If you had to portray somebody who did not harbor resentment against commercial stereotypes, could you do it? If you are a good actress, you could.

If you cannot, absolutely will not get your head around this, then I think it would be a wise move not to get involved with commercials at all. The ad agency people will see right through you when they replay the tapes, and you will just be in for a lot of frustration. Life is too short to do things that you really don't want to do.

Commercials are the very last medium to reflect changes in mores and fashions. First, societal change shows up in the movies or on stage, then on television shows, and finally in commercials. They tend to reflect a view of the world that is idealized, sanitized to the point of fantasy. The last thing Madison Avenue wants to do is offend somebody with adventuresome, real-world commercials.

Just to give you an idea of how conservative they really are, consider the following taboos: you never see toilet paper next to the toilet in commercials. Ever notice? It can be rolling down the steps or getting squeezed in a market, but it never appears where it actually goes. Douche commercials never precisely mention what a douche is used for; you never see an actual picture of a tampon; you never see anybody actually drink hard liquor, and you never see anybody swallow an aspirin or any other kind of pill.

But don't confuse conservative with stupid. The people who create and produce commercials know exactly what they are doing. Market research is their middle name, and if they are conservative in their approach it is only because they know for certain that that is the best way to sell the product.

I once read a *Wall Street Journal* article about the degree of market research done in advertising. It involved a study done by the McCann-Erickson advertising agency in which they tried to determine why the female consumer prefers spray-can roach killers to the "roach hotel" variety. According to the article, women will buy the spray even if they believe the "hotel" to be a superior product.

So the agency got a group of women together and asked them to draw pictures of roaches—with their left hands. Since the right hemisphere of the brain is visual, symbolic, and emotional, and controls the left half of the body, drawing with the left hand taps into perceptions better. Then, after the pictures of roaches were drawn, the women were asked to write a little story explaining how they felt about the roaches. Well, surprise number one was that every single woman drew *male* roaches (I don't know, maybe they had on little ties or something), not female ones, so the ad agency figured all of this was symbolic of male-female relationships. Surprise number two was that, in the stories, it became clear that the women liked to watch the roaches squirm and die! A roach hotel might be a kinder, gentler , more effective product, but the user wouldn't get the kind of emotional satisfaction from it that she would from a spray.

The article went on to discuss female fears of male abandonment and such, but you get the idea. The point is that these folks are thorough when it comes to devising TV ads. Why, I have even done commercials for products that don't exist. The agency will make a sample product, the total output of which is on the commercial set. Then they'll do a spot and put it on the air in a test market like Oklahoma City, following up with phone calls to randomly selected TV viewers. If enough people answer the survey questions the right way, then the manufacturer will go ahead and make some of the product to sell. This is a cheaper procedure than gearing up for manufacture first.

HOW COMMERCIALS ARE CAST

Once a casting director has instructions from an ad agency, he or she puts out calls to talent agents, who suggest actors. Audition times are scheduled, and actors show up at the casting studio, where their auditions are put on videotape. Usually, only the actor and casting director are present at this first audition. After that, the tape is reviewed by the ad agency creative team, the director, and the client (the people who make the product); they whittle the list of original actors down to a handful who are asked to come to a "callback." At the callback, they repeat what they did at the first audition, again being videotaped. The difference is that this time, the actual director is there to give adjustments.

Casting decisions are made from this callback audition, except on the rare occasion when yet another callback is scheduled. As a rule, the commercial is shot within a week.

One high-tech variation that you might encounter if you live in a major urban center is the video-conference casting session. Here, actors audition live for decision makers who may be a continent away. I went to one in San Francisco, reading for the producers and directors who were watching me from their office in Chicago. It's weird, but it works. The technology for this kind of casting session is still too expensive for it to really catch on, but we'll probably see more of it in time.

Regarding what to wear to a commercial audition, both men and women should stick with pastels, muted colors, earth tones. Stay away from busy patterns, paisleys, that kind of thing. Also, avoid shirts or sweaters that are solid red, white, or black, because those colors draw attention away from your face.

Women should have in their wardrobes a number of sweater-shirt combinations and some skirts. Slacks are fine if they aren't too tight. A business suit is a necessity, particularly if you are thirty or older. Sportswear is a definite yes. At a minimum, you should have the type of sportswear that you might put on to go bike riding or jogging. Jeans can be okay at times, but be careful. I would advise against them unless you know for certain they are appropriate.

Men should also have some sweater-shirt combos and some slacks. Chinos are great. Plaids or pastels are good. A blue blazer and slacks are a wonderfully flexible outfit. A nice business suit is good to have. With sportswear, the same thing goes for men as for women.

Everybody should avoid dangling jewelry, things that catch the light.

WORKING WITH VIDEOTAPE

Virtually all commercial auditions are recorded on videotape, a factor that distinguishes them immediately from the "live" auditions held for TV shows, movies, and stage. Videotape didn't appear until about 1970, but in just a few years it revolutionized the world of commercials.

- FACT: Videotape makes it possible for the ad agency to tap into a national talent pool. Actors in San Francisco and

Orlando now routinely audition for commercials that originate in New York or L.A.

- FACT: Videotape has created a whole new job category, that of the independent casting director. There needs to be some way technically to reach the talent pools in the cities of America, and the freelance casting director is part of the equation.
- FACT: Videotape positively must be mastered as a medium by anyone who seriously wants to act in commercials. You may be a wonderful stage actor, but you can still get befuddled by videotape cameras.
- FACT: Videotape puts a barrier between actors and their potential employers. Auditioning on tape is quite a different situation than being able to walk in and shake hands with the nice people.

I have seen many fine actors turn to mush in front of a videotape camera. It's not like working in a movie, where you rarely look directly into the lens of the camera. Suddenly, you are expected to not only look into the lens, but to relate to it, all the while maintaining a chipper and energetic demeanor. Some people behave as though they have met their first Martian and basically would rather be in Philadelphia.

The camera tells the truth, nothing more and nothing less. It doesn't amplify things, and it doesn't make you look different than you do in life. Maybe it is because people sense this that they want to withdraw from the scrutiny. It can be embarrassing to have the truth about you shown on a TV screen. And, of course, as soon as you begin to withdraw, that becomes the reality that the camera sees, and when the ad agency people replay the tape later, they see an actor who doesn't want to be there. Why hire that person?

Good news: if the videotape camera is the dragon of your worst nightmares, you'll be happy to learn that the dragon can definitely be tamed. It is possible to come across on camera as warm and personable. How? By personalizing the camera. That means you have to develop the craft of being able to talk to a camera as if it might talk back to you.

New people as well as experienced actors frequently have the mistaken notion that, when you talk into the lens of the camera, you should be performing a commercial for the camera to take a picture of. They equate it roughly to the transaction that took place when Mom used to point the Brownie and instruct them to say cheese. This is not that. Talking into a videotape camera at a commercial audition is a one-of-a-kind thing. You are not performing for the camera, and you are not talking to "America." What you are doing is trying to make it seem like you are talking to each *individual* person who is watching the replay or the commercial, and the way you do that is to pretend that the camera is one person.

Children have no trouble at all with this concept. In fact, they love it. I taught a group of kids once and was fascinated by the ways they would play with the camera. "Pretend the camera is Mom," I would tell them. "Okay!" they would respond. "Where's Dad?" For them, it was just a game. But adults have learned to be inhibited and have learned what it means to be embarrassed. They are afraid they will look silly if they talk to a camera as if it is a person who might talk back. "I wouldn't dance with a mop in the middle of Hollywood Boulevard, and I won't talk to a camera as if it is a person who might talk back," they seem to say.

I'm going to ask you to do something that you may never have done before, and I think it will help you understand the kind of transaction that is necessary between you and the videotape camera.

Look around the room you are sitting in right at this moment until you find something small and inanimate that you can relate to. That light switch over by the door will do just fine. Now, tell the light switch hello. Go ahead, do it. Don't worry about being silly. Just look right at the light switch, smile, and say "Hello!" Did it react to you? It did? Well, then you need to see a doctor. Light switches don't react, and wishing won't make it so. But—are you ready?—you can *pretend* that it did! You can pretend that, when you said hello, the light switch grinned, flipped its little toggle, and said "Hiya!" right back. Now you in turn react to the light switch's greeting. If you really want to test the relationship you have with your new friend, go ahead and tell him about the wonderful time you had on your last vacation. Pretend that he is loving the story, is eager to hear more. Build up to the most exciting part, the moment when you met Mr. or Ms. Right walking on the beach. You are happy, the light switch is happy, everybody is happy! Okay, the exercise is complete. If the light switch had been a videotape camera at an audition, you would have been relating correctly. You see? It isn't the same thing as talking *at* the light switch; you have to talk *with* it, to communicate with it.

Words express a thought, right? You can also express a thought with a kiss or a kick in the shin or a bear hug. The important thing is that expressing a thought implies the presence of another person—you need somebody to express *to*. That other person at a commercial audition is frequently the camera. When you begin talking to another person, you check his or her reaction to what you are saying so that you can tell how to proceed. That is why the punchline is at the end of the joke rather than at the beginning. You start telling the joke and, watching to be sure the person is following you, you build up to the punchline. If you were talking to a person and saw a look of noncomprehension, you'd have to drop back and rephrase what you just said before you could move forward.

I realize it is a little awkward to dissect communication in this fashion, but it is the easiest way to learn how to relate to an inanimate object like a camera. In life, we don't usually inspect the way we communicate on a frame-by-frame basis, but it can be a useful exercise in this context.

Are there any exceptions? The only one I can think of is something comedic. I have seen a few commercials where the actors are purposely doing a parody of someone who does not relate to the camera, someone like a game show host or a newscaster. TV newspeople are frequently too busy reading the TelePrompTer to relate to the camera. And, of course, game show hosts are notorious for slickness and noninvolvement. They paste on a big plastic smile, look right into the camera, and talk to A-M-E-R-I-C-A! But, as I say, the exceptions are few. You'll be safe if you presume that you should always relate to the camera unless a specific situation demands otherwise.

Now, in commercials that involve couples or groups of people acting out situations, the camera becomes an audience to the scene, and the actors should not look at it. The thing to remember is that, if you look directly into the lens of the camera, it breaks the "fourth wall." When you do it, you are bringing the person who is watching the TV right into the scene with you, just the same as if you turned around on stage and addressed the fellow on the front row.

For example, if you are reading for a spot in which a husband and wife are in the bathroom discussing toothpaste, you certainly wouldn't want to address the camera. If you did, you would bring a third person into the bathroom with you. The same thing would be true for a romantic spot on a deserted Hawaiian beach. There isn't anybody else out there, and if you talk to the camera, you break the illusion.

But you can do an "aside" just the way you would in the theater. In fact, it can be extremely effective. Suppose the situation involved a bunch of people sitting quietly in a library reading room. Suddenly, this fellow starts munching on chips. "Crunch!" The script may only indicate that the guy next to him is supposed to be surprised, that he should jump and be startled. It would be absolutely wonderful to do a slow "take" to camera in such a case. It would be okay because we are in a place where there are a lot of people and, theoretically, the viewer at home is one of them. Get it?

And then, of course, there is always the situation where it is written in the script that everybody on camera relates to the camera. There are lots of spots like this. Just remember that the camera is *one* person.

The main challenge when working with other people on camera is to make sure you are seen in as many planes as possible. In life, you might stand toe to toe when talking to your friend, but if you do that on camera, you'll only be seen in profile. Instead, you have to "cheat" out. Instead of toe to toe, stand shoulder to shoulder at a slight angle to the camera.

Having said all of this, I guarantee that you will encounter situations where the casting director will tell you point blank that he wants you to look into the camera on a particular line, and you will know full well that it is inappropriate to do it. I would rather see you get the job and get paid than be right, so don't snicker and don't argue. Let the casting directors do their job. They may have their own reasons for wanting you to look into the camera. Maybe the folks at the ad agency asked for it.

You have to know what is correct technique, how perspective and point of view work. That way, if you run into an exception, you'll treat it as just that, and you'll return to a firm base with the next audition.

"RESULT" DIRECTION

At commercial auditions, you are going to get a kind of direction that you rarely get at auditions for stage, movies, or television shows—"result" direction. What that means is that the casting director is going to tell you the precise "result" he or she wants to see in your audition, saying, for example, "Make it animated," "Warm it up, lots of eyes," "Play it macho," "Be broad, have fun with it," "They're looking for big facial reactions on this one."

An experienced theatrical director will usually give an actor "situational" direction; in fact, it is a sign of weakness to resort to asking for "results." He or she will set up the situation for you, perhaps suggest an objective, and then let you play it as you will, changing the objective or some circumstance in order to alter your performance if necessary. For example, a seasoned director might set up a situation this way: "You've just arrived at your home and discover the front door is ajar. You push it open and enter, only to discover the furniture in disarray. Your spouse is nowhere to be seen, and the place is quiet. Suddenly, you hear an object fall on the floor upstairs. Go and see what it is." Result direction for the same situation would be: "You've just arrived home and discover the front door is ajar. Tense up as you slowly push the door open to discover the furniture in disarray. Big shocked expression on your face. Suddenly, you hear an object fall on the floor upstairs. Freeze in your steps. Look to your left and right. Then, quietly go see what the noise was. You should be very fearful and anxious."

The reason that casting directors for commercials so frequently give this kind of direction is that they take their instructions from ad agency people and, as we have already discussed, these people are not in the entertainment business at all. The ad agency's producer may tell the casting director that he or she is looking for several actors who are "broadly animated," for example, and the casting director will carry that right into the audition. Rather than direct situationally, he or she will say, "Lots of animation on this . . . big faces, the bigger the better . . . very broad . . . have fun with it."

Lesson number one in any basic acting class is that you cannot act a "result." It is impossible to act "animation," and it is impossible to act "broad." If you try to do it, you'll only succeed in making faces for no reason at all; your acting will be unmotivated. The fact is that acting means *doing* something. You have to pursue objectives, play specific actions.

Clearly, I can't teach someone to act in a few paragraphs. If this concept of "results" versus "actions" is alien to you, I strongly suggest you get yourself into a good acting workshop. Understanding this type of thing is precisely what separates the nonactor from the professional, and it is the primary reason the bulk of the jobs go to the pros. If you don't know how to convert "result" direction to something active, you'll be almost totally dependent on your physical type and winning personality to get you cast in commercials. That may do the trick some of the time, but you'll be operating at a decided disadvantage.

For now, here are a couple of sample "result" directions and suggested response to them.

I'm at an audition for Burger King, and the situation calls for me to eat a burger and say to the camera, "Now, that's a good burger!" I do it once, and the casting director says, "Do it again. Much more energy. Much broader." I do a second take and this time pretend that I've been on the desert for the past week with no food to eat. I'm famished. I dig into the burger with all my heart, and "Now, that's a good burger!" comes out with twice the gusto as before. I didn't try to play broader or with more energy. What I did was raise the stakes situationally. Get it?

I'm at an audition for an antiperspirant product, straight spokesman material. I give it my best shot, and the casting director says I should "warm it up. More one-to-one." I do a second take, this time pretending that I am talking to a woman instead of a man. The net result is a warmer reading.

The trick is to listen to what the casting director tells you and then to translate that into something that is playable. That's your job, it's what they pay you for. A casting director really isn't there to teach you how to act, and the concept of playing an action will ideally be second nature to you.

PREPARING FOR THE AUDITION

When you arrive at the casting studio, fill out the SAG sign-in sheet on the table (yes, even if you're not in SAG, fill it out), pick up a copy of the script from the stack next to the sign-in sheet, and glance around to see if there is a storyboard taped to the wall.

A storyboard is a cartoon depiction of the commercial. It looks like a black-and-white version of the Sunday comics with each panel representing a different shot of the commercial. Not every commercial has a storyboard at the audition, and you don't absolutely have to have one, but they can be helpful. Commercial copy sometimes appears oblique unless you know what the visuals will be.

You'll have five to fifty minutes before you'll be called into the audition room. If they keep you longer than an hour, the casting director gets reprimanded by SAG, so these things tend to move along. Expect to spend about fifteen minutes on average.

There are various kinds of commercials you are likely to encounter. For a spot with copy, on camera alone (very common), you stand all by yourself and talk directly to the camera. A spot with copy, on camera with a group, might encompass anything from a football stadium full of people to a husband and wife in the bathroom. For a spot with no copy, on camera alone or with a group (also very common), you will usually be doing an improvisational audition (See "Improvisational Auditions," page 58).

The first thing to do is to read the spot carefully. Be sure you can pronounce everything and that you understand every single sentence and nuance. If in doubt, ask the casting director during one of his trips to the waiting room. Next, categorize the commercial in terms of style. Is it a pie-in-the-face slapstick kind of thing? Is it a warm puppy dog? Slice-of-life? Straight spokesperson? Who is the target audience? Women? Teens? This information will help you when trying to figure out who you might be talking to when you look into the camera. What kind of advertising claims are being made about the product? What are they saying is special about it? Remember, advertising is about getting people to buy product A instead of product B on the premise that they'll buy something from this product category anyway. Most commercials contain an implied comparison.

Now you're ready to begin looking at the copy from a first-person perspective. The thought process goes: "Okay, what am I [not what is the character] doing in this spot?" Own it. Ask yourself these questions:

- "Where am I?" In other words, what is the location of the commercial? Does it take place in a parking lot? In a bedroom? At a soccer game?
- "Who am I talking to?" What is my relationship with him or her? If you are talking to the camera, who is it? Remember, you can't talk to "America." With some copy there may be no clue at all, so you'll have to impose it.
- If you are on camera with other people, who are they? Do you know them, or are they strangers? Relationship is everything, and the more specific you are about it, the better. A husband-wife relationship calls for intimacy of the fanny-slapping variety right from the start, for instance. Why am I telling my girlfriend about this detergent? Why am I buying this new TV set?

Why are we at the restaurant? Is it our anniversary or just a casual date? Again, you may well have to impose choices of this sort because many commercials don't even give a clue.

- If there is no dialogue, no copy, then what are my actions? Why am I doing what I'm doing? Motivate, motivate, motivate!

All right, you've answered all of the questions. Now you can start rehearsing. I personally think the best way is to speak the words out loud if there are any. Go find a light switch to talk to, or go out in the parking lot and chat with a car. Do anything except sit there and meditate on it. If you have a two-person spot, you might want to run over it with the other actor, but the problem is that you can't be sure who that is. The casting director may very well already have you matched up on a list, so you can't presume that you will be reading with the next person on the sign-in sheet. Therefore, you may not be able to rehearse with the other actor. Anyway, some actors don't like to rehearse with others in waiting rooms. They like to save all of the surprises and juice for the camera. If you know for sure who will be reading with you, go ahead and ask if he or she wants to rehearse. If the person demurs, don't be offended.

When rehearsing, stay away from mirrors! This is another of those items that is the subject of much bad advice. I've heard many supposedly knowledgeable individuals tell aspiring actors that they specifically should rehearse in front of mirrors, and it merely is an indication that the advice-giver really doesn't understand what actors do. The fact is that you can't be on the stage and in the audience simultaneously, right? If you're on the stage and you want to be in the audience, you have to walk down those little steps to get there. That's reality. When you rehearse in front of a mirror, you are trying to force an impossible issue: you're trying to be both actor and audience at the same time. You're acting and watching yourself to see how you're doing.

You can always tell which actors have been rehearsing in front of mirrors because when they get into the audition room, they have terminal cases of the "cutes." They stand in the bathroom and work out where to wink and smile and giggle, and then they come into the audition room and try to re-create what they did in the bathroom! That's not acting, that's mimicry. And, anyway, if you try to do it, you'll only hurt yourself as an actor. Keep the process conceptual: "Where am I? Who am I talking to? Why am I telling him this?"

MEMORIZING AND CUE CARDS

Anybody who has ever done one-week stock knows that memorizing is a learned skill. After a summer spent rehearsing one play in the daytime, performing another one at night, and then changing plays every week, you get to the point where you go to breakfast and walk away having memorized the menu! You train yourself to accomplish a kind of surface-level memorization, and as soon as the summer is over, all of it vanishes from your brain.

At commercial auditions, you don't have to memorize the copy unless you want to. They will have a nice big piece of poster board right next to the camera with the words printed on it in magic marker. SAG has a rule about this, and the casting director can actually face a union reprimand if a cue card is not in use for a commercial that has copy. All you have to do is relate to the camera, and when you forget what comes next, glance over at the cue card, get the words, and bring them back to camera.

As easy a process as this seems, I see actors get thrown by cue cards all the time. Because the words are right there in their faces, they seem to feel compelled not to make a single mistake. Rather than concentrate on the logic of the piece, they worry about the words, longing to stare at the card and afraid that it will look odd on camera if they do. The cue card therefore becomes a kind of distraction rather than an aid.

The easiest thing to do is simply to memorize the copy and be done with it. Anyway, you get a small competitive edge if you do. If you are skittish about it, however, you'll only cripple your audition by pressuring yourself to memorize. You may have the copy firmly in your head in the waiting room and then, under pressure of the actual audition, it evaporates; you wind up standing there looking at the camera while scanning an internal script. On replay, you can see a fixed look in the eyes rather than the warmth of communication. It comes across as a variation on self-doubt.

If you want to learn to memorize quickly, get in the practice of finding the logic of the copy right away. When you pick up the script in the waiting room, resist the temptation to start memorizing right away. If you get the logic first, you'll find the words in the copy are the only ones that will make sense. That way, even if you get something wrong, you'll go right back on track because you understand the points you need to make. This kind of memorization isn't like learning the books of the Bible or a grocery list. There is a flow to it.

If you are really bothered by the idea, however, try this compromise: Commit the first thought—whether it's one, two, or three lines—to memory. That way, after you slate your name and "action" is called, you won't begin your audition by looking at a card instead of the camera. You'll involve the viewer immediately. Then, refer to the card in the middle of the spot, even if you have to read that entire section. At the end, have the last thought in your memory for a strong finish.

You need not make yourself crazy over each comma and period in the copy. If you mess up a little, nobody will hold it against you unless you kick yourself for it. Just don't rewrite the spot. The ad agency people understand that auditions are tough, that you may not have had very long with the script before reading, and they figure you'll get it memorized correctly by the time you are hired and on the set. This isn't an invitation to engage in wholesale paraphrasing, only permission to be human.

One more thing: when you are standing in front of the camera, it can feel like you are shifting your gaze from New York to Paris when you go back and forth between the camera and the cue card. It may seem like that at the time, but it doesn't look that way on replay, so don't worry about it.

THE AUDITIONING PROCESS

You'll usually find yourself alone in the audition room with the casting director, sometimes with a camera operator. There will be some simple but bright lighting and a videotape setup.

The casting director will guide you to your "mark" (the place where you stand) and tell you what he or she wants you to do in the audition. If it involves any blocking, this is where that will be made clear. This is also the time to ask any questions you have about the spot.

Take a moment to read the cue card even if you are confident that you have memorized the copy. Because it is written with magic markers, there are fewer words per line than the typewritten script and, if you have to refer to it during the reading, you don't want to be searching around for your place. Also, the announcer's lines that you see in the commercial script will usually not be written on the cue card in the audition room because those lines are not spoken aloud in the audition. The exception would be if the actor on camera has to react to an off-camera speaker.

If your reading involves a "now and later" situation, the casting director will usually stop the camera to allow for a passage of time. For instance, the "now" part may involve two girls talking about how awful their hair looks, and the "later" part takes place after the hero product has been used.

The casting director may want you to rehearse once before turning on the tape but, if he or she knows your work, might just tape the rehearsal. Personally, I don't like to rehearse these things unless there is a lot of complicated physical business like pouring coffee and holding up products.

When you're ready, the tape machine is turned on and the casting director asks you to "slate your name," to look into the lens and say who you are. Treat it like a warm handshake, an introduction, not like chalk on a blackboard. And for God's sake, pronounce your name clearly! It is a terrible thing to witness how mushy-mouthed some people get with their own names.

Then you'll get one or two takes, and that will be that. The casting director thanks you; you return to the waiting room and sign out.

HANDLING PRODUCTS AND EATING FOOD

The only thing to remember about handling a product is not to wave it around while you are talking and to drop it away when you don't want to show it anymore. If you can, keep the product close to your face and try to position it so the camera can see the product name. Rather than hoisting up the product à la the Statue of Liberty, track the camera's "eyes" to make sure it is seeing what you are trying to display. The camera is a person, remember? Well, when you show somebody something, you track their eyes to make sure they saw it. This kind of nuance is what really gives an audition color and credibility.

If you are auditioning for a fast-food spot, you may well have to eat something. Hopefully, it will be something real, but if it isn't, be prepared to pretend to eat. This is a skill you *can* work on in front of a mirror. In fact, I spend time in my workshops doing nothing except working with actors on how to eat imaginary food. If they have crackers or something, which is often the case, just remember this: you are doing an audition for a food product, so it would help if you eat with gusto. Let the client think that, if it comes down to a choice between eating his wonderful product and talking, eating will almost always win out. Let the food delight you.

IMPROVISATIONAL AUDITIONS

There are two basic kinds of improvisational auditions, *situational* and *sense-of-life*. A situational improv audition involves a setup of some kind, and the actor is expected actually to perform a scene. The sense-of-life audition involves nothing more than standing in front of the camera, giving a nice name slate, perhaps chatting with the casting director while the tape is rolling, and that's it. They may ask you to talk about your last vacation or your favorite food or something—just to make conversation. If you get either of those kinds of auditions, you can be sure that physical type is the primary consideration, so all you can do is be nice, have fun with the audition process, and try not to feel bad if you don't get cast.

Situational improv auditions need a little bit of discussion. As an example, I'll describe a fairly typical one that I went to, a spot for one of those stores that provides anything and everything for the do-it-yourselfer. The spot was divided into three parts, beginning with Our Hero (me) shopping and then trying to go through checkout with all the boxes. Then Our Hero and The Wife are industriously hammering and painting a room; finally, they enjoy a moment of closeness as they survey their handiwork. Music up, fade out.

The casting director was shooting the audition in three setups, cutting between each. All he wanted to see on the first part was a shopper buying more stuff than he could rightly carry. On "action," I elected to bobble the boxes, dropping one and trying to pick it up while laughing at my awkwardness. Finally succeeding, I walked out of frame as we cut. The next section called for building something with the wife. The casting director said, "Okay, you two are busy. Ed, you are hammering and Claudia, you're painting. You are both into the task." Mind you, he never said what we were building, but I didn't really expect him to. In my mind, it was a nursery for the new baby. That choice gave me a nice positive initiative to build and a reason to smile meaningfully at Claudia. I don't know what she was playing, but she smiled back. The last part involved us contentedly surveying what we had built. Rather than stand there like a rock, I chose to point out the place in the wall above the camera where I nailed up my secret creation.

Now, I've outlined my personal choices to give you an idea of how much latitude you have in an improv audition. With no dialogue to guide you and minimal situational direction, you need to fill in a lot of blanks.

Another example: A spot for a hamburger chain. This one calls for Our Hero to arrive at the outlet, to stand in line, and then to place his order with an elderly counterman. Hero is surprised to see an oldster back there instead of the usual teenager. Cut. Then, in the second part, Hero happily eats his burger as we watch the oldster industriously serving more customers in the background. Music up.

My choice for the first part was, number one, to arrive hungry and, number two, for this to be my very favorite place to eat. I made sure I was in a really excellent humor, pretending that I just that morning landed a part in a movie. Suddenly, there was the oldster. Why, I *know* that guy! He lives right down my block! I laughed and bantered with him. Then in the second part, I eat and reflect on what a nice discovery it was to see Old James working here at my favorite place.

Are you getting the idea? Motivate, motivate, motivate! Go for relationships. Do something. Give yourself actions to play even if the casting director doesn't provide them. In the fast-food spot, nobody said anything about me knowing the oldster. The direction was, "You're surprised but pleased. Nice warm smile . . ." That is not an active direction, so I gave it substance.

It's okay to talk, shout, or make noise unless you are specifically told not to. A lot of actors make the mistake of turning into Marcel Marceau at these improv auditions. If they ask you to slate your name, you know they are recording sound, so go ahead and make noise if it is appropriate to the situation. Remember that you are not being judged on your wit. In fact, there will be no dialogue at all in the final script. It's okay if your words are corny or even strange.

Find ways to animate your body during the audition. It looks much more interesting than simply standing there. All of us humans are more influenced by what we see than by what we hear. And try to imagine what the music track for the spot will be, and match your audition dynamic to it. They are going to cast people to match their music.

For the *sense-of-life* audition, you slate your name and chat with the casting director. Some actors get hives over this and hate to be scrutinized in this way. Remember, the only reason they are chatting with you is to have a reason to keep the camera on for a moment. Since the final spot obviously doesn't involve a situation that requires audition, they are focusing on type, so they just want to look at you. It's not a test, so relax. Nothing is expected of you.

It's not unusual to have the casting director ask, "What have you been up to lately?" or "Tell us about yourself," open-ended questions that could be answered in any number of ways. Keep your responses brief and bright. If you can, try to be theatrically relevant. Tell him you've been auditioning a lot lately (even if it's not true), or mention the play you're rehearsing. If you have zero theatrical activity to talk about, then tell him about your last vacation or how you've been training your dog. The important thing is not to drone on and look defensive. The questions do not have right and wrong answers, and the only reason he asked them was to see you on camera for a minute or so. It is not an invitation to go into a ramble about how you were born poor and found your way to the big city.

As with a situational improv, animate yourself physically if at all possible. Try to imagine how the audition might look if they played it back with the sound off. Would you simply be there talking, never changing your expression or stance?

A special note to actors who live in cities other than New York, Hollywood, and Chicago: I realize that you have a day job and may not get as much theatrical activity as you want yet. Still, if asked to talk about yourself in an improv audition, keep in mind that this casting session might be going on in several cities at once, and your competition might be full-time actors. Therefore, avoid approaches like "Well, I've been working at the Bank of America for twelve years in the accounting department, but I'm not very happy, so I hope to get into acting." Or, "Now that I've been laid off by the phone company, I was thinking that commercials might be a good thing to do." If you don't have anything else to talk about, mention acting classes you are taking. And, again, be happy about it!

THE CALLBACK AUDITION

If you are called back, you will be going through the same audition a second time, now being directed by the actual director, probably in the presence of the ad agency team and the client.

Casting decisions at this point are highly subjective, a game of mix and match, of balancing type and personal chemistry. Physical characteristics such as family resemblance, hair color, and height take on great significance, and all of the actors there can technically do the spot or they wouldn't have been called back.

The director may give you direction that is radically different from what you had in your initial audition. If so, just go with whatever he or she says. Remember, the director is showing off a bit for his or her boss, the ad agency producer, and wants to put his or her stamp on you. Try to make the director look good.

Try to wear the same clothes you wore to the first audition. It's hard to know precisely what they are responding to in you, but it's best for them to see the same package that was on the tape walk into the room.

When you enter the room, you'll see all these people just kind of sitting around awkwardly. They may laugh nervously or outright ignore you. Make eye contact if you can, put them at ease. Pretend the audition is being held in your living room, and they have all come over to visit you on your terms. Those are the ad agency people and client, and they won't relax until later when they review the tape again.

If they start a mix-and-match process with you and the other actors in the waiting room, you can be certain it is all a matter of chemistry and complementary types. Your talent isn't on the line, so relax. Whenever they team you up with another new partner, bend your performance to accommodate whatever he is doing. Try not to freeze your performance even if you have to go in and out of the room ten times.

The single biggest mistake actors make at callback is figuring they should re-create whatever they did at the first audition. Forget it. You can't do it. That performance is history. Even if the director says, "We like what you did, just do that again," you can't do it. Play in the present moment. Make it fresh. Anyway, if you worry about trying to re-create what you did before, you'll just make yourself nervous.

HELPFUL HINTS

After many years of teaching commercial audition technique, I have seen certain problem areas arise again and again. This list isn't meant to be all inclusive, but it will point you in the right direction. Read it before your next commercial audition.

- Your audition begins the moment you enter the room, not the moment the camera is turned on. Get yourself into gear early.
- Deal with mistakes with humor. Never apologize for a flubbed take. Unless a take has been blown beyond repair, try to improvise and save it. Once you abort a take, the casting director will have to rewind the videotape machine, finding the starting point of your audition all over again. This process is time consuming and builds tension. It also creates pressure on the actor to get it right the next time. Better to fix it the first time, even if that involves paraphrasing or improvisational damage control.
- It is not the actor's job to sell the product. That job belongs to the ad agency. What you want to do is convey your delight at having discovered the product. Share that discovery with the camera.
- Husband-wife relationships are frequently played as mother-son relationships in commercials, especially if you are selling household products.
- Mentally bring the camera to you when you look at it, rather than "chasing" it. In the first place, it makes you appear more confident, and in the second, the camera operator has probably zoomed in a bit. Even though the camera may be twelve feet away from you in reality, it will look like five or six on replay.
- Never try to play your type. This is a particular problem for beautiful, sexy, and handsome folks. The reasoning goes: "I'm here for a sexy spot, so I am supposed to behave in a sexy manner." No. Let your type take care of that. You can't act handsome or sexy anyway.
- Pretend advertising claims are true. I love this one and use it all the time. As consumers, we are as cynical as everybody else and realize that commercial claims are frequently so much hot air. But what if they were true? Wouldn't they be worth talking about with enthusiasm? Suppose this new brand of pantyhose really was both durable and sheer? Suppose it were true instead of advertising blabber, wouldn't it be swell? Pretend it is true, and act accordingly.

- Pretend you personally invented the product and/or the product demonstration. It will give you more of a stake.

- The videotape camera can be your friend or your enemy. If it is your friend, you'll be glad to see it at each audition. You'll have an ally in the room.
- A sigh is almost always a sign of personal pain and is practically never appropriate to commercials. Usually, actors sigh in auditions because they are nervous and in great discomfort. Sighing only highlights it, so don't.
- Commercials frequently involve cartoon critters—dancing raisins, talking pats of butter, and voices that come out of the sky. In life, such occurrences would cause you to run screaming from the house; in commercials, all the little creatures are your buddies! Make friends with them. Let them delight you.
- When you are on camera alone, remember that you are usually bringing up the subject. The camera didn't ask. Speak with initiative, with intent to make a point.
- When working with another actor on camera, stand closer than you would in real life. Nobody likes strangers right up in their face, but you won't look too close on replay.
- Don't be afraid to physically touch another actor on camera.
- Always be ready to reverse roles.
- Never be skeptical about the advertising claims of the hero product—inquisitive, studious, but never negative.
- If the spot is for a food product, you can't go wrong by nibbling on it.
- Never direct the other actor, even if his or her performance is awful. Let the casting director do it.
- Your acting choices should be bold enough to cost you the job. I wish I had a dime for every actor who, on his way back to his seat said, "Well, I wanted to do that, but I thought it would be too much."
- Remember, life was going on before the first line of copy, and it continues after the last line of copy. Don't end an audition with a "freeze frame."
- It's okay to add a "button," a short ad lib, at the end of a spot if the situation merits it. If the husband's last line in a spot was "Honey, you're the best wife in the world," it would be a good button to say, "Yeah, I know" or "And you're the best husband." The ad agency doesn't mind this at all as a rule, and if they do, they'll tell you.
- If you are auditioning for a "spokesperson" role, say for a

bank or an insurance company, you can still be warm and personal when you relate to the camera. Institutions of that sort are viewed with suspicion by large segments of the population, and they are looking for actors who will create an image of accessibility. Let your business suit define you as corporate. Keep your performance down to earth. Don't be afraid to use humor, even with the driest copy.

CHAPTER 5

Auditioning for
Voice Work

The phrase "voice work" is actually a convenient umbrella term that covers a garden variety of jobs. A partial list would include radio commercials, computer games, off-camera voices for TV commercials, narration for educational and industrial films, voices in animated cartoons and TV series, recordings of novels, and background voices ("walla") in movies and TV shows.

Actors' voices are needed to announce floors in some elevators, to navigate phone mazes for us ("push 3 for accounting, push 4 for legal . . ."). They even tell us the time and advise us to buckle up in the car. When you start counting, the uses for actors' voices represent a considerable amount of employment.

The lion's share of the jobs in this field go to a relatively small group of performers, not because they are more talented than the rest of us, but because this is a highly specialized field. On-camera production may continue until the sun goes down, but when producers want to record voices, they rent recording studios by the hour. The working voice-over professional can step up to the mike, toss off four or five variations of a script one after the other, and be done in a couple of hours. He or she is able to make the reading warmer or happier or more corporate if the director in the control booth asks for it, and knows precisely how far from the microphone to place the mouth, how to breathe in the right places, and what to do if there is a problem with "popping." ("Popping" is when consonant sounds such as the "p" in peanut and the "t" in technical are too hard, too sharp. On replay, the explosion of breath sounds like a "pop." The remedy is to move your mouth slightly off to the side of the mike when recording.)

If a newcomer wants to do on-camera commercials, it is only

necessary to be a good commercial type, to have a happy sense-of-life, and to be willing to follow simple direction. As already discussed, it is not uncommon for nonactors—folks with zero theatrical background—to work on-camera in commercials. But if that same newcomer wants to work in voice overs, the learning curve is more notable. A nonpro will find it tough going indeed. It is not enough merely to have a pleasant speaking voice and clear diction.

To further illustrate how specialized this field can be, consider the workshop I took some years ago in Los Angeles. It was being conducted at the Mullholand Drive home of a major voice talent, a woman whose voice you have heard hundreds of times. All of the students had at least some experience with a mike. I had, for my part, already done a number of radio commercials and TV voice overs. Well, this woman put on a remarkable show of talent that day. First she created the voice of a cartoon munchkin, a cute, fluffy kind of little furry guy. Then she immediately created the voice of the munchkin's wife. And, finally, she created his two children, each with a distinctive munchkin voice. All of the munchkins were clearly of the same family, but they were each distinguishable, each unique. We were, to put it mildly, impressed.

HOW VOICE CASTING WORKS

Depending on the kind of project, voice casting can happen a number of different ways. The producer may hire an independent casting director who will call talent agents and conduct auditions similar to those you would encounter at an on-camera commercial audition. The major difference is that the actors are in a recording booth when they audition, and there is no videotape camera.

The producer might skip the casting director altogether, thereby saving some money, and communicate directly with talent agents who represent voice-over talent. Virtually all agents who are active in this field have mini-recording booths in their offices; when they get a casting call, they prepare an agency tape for submission to the producer. The talent agent earns money via commissions on the work his or her performer-clients get. Or the producer may function as a casting director, calling miscellaneous agents and having each of them send their performers to his or her office for auditions.

I have even heard of a situation in which a software company conducted a casting session for a children's CD-ROM over the telephone! The in-house casting director for the company called a local hotline that was maintained by a nonprofit theatrical organization and described what kind of voices he was seeking. Interested performers called a number and did their audition from home. The producer later brought the finalists into his company recording studio for a face-to-face reading.

And, finally, it is entirely possible to be cast with no audition at all, especially if you have a really hot demo tape. A producer listens to your tape, hears the precise voice he or she is looking for, and bingo!—you get a call to meet at the recording studio. It happens.

"WALLA"

Walla is the oddly named job for actors who provide background crowd noises in movies and TV shows. For example, let's say a movie scene has been shot in a bus terminal. The stars of the movie sit on a bench and talk about the prison riot that just happened. During actual filming, extras in the terminal were directed to move around silently so that the principal performers' dialogue could be heard and recorded on a clean track. Once the scene is developed and ready for editing, it is projected on to a screen in a special kind of recording studio—to add background voices. Walla performers watch it and then record voices for those extras who are moving around in the bus station. Then the walla voices are edited into the final sound track so that the viewing audience will get the impression that all of the sound was recorded at the same time. Movie magic.

I remember shooting a TV movie scene in which I was dancing with the female star in a square-dance kind of setting. We were doing the Texas Two Step and talking about autopsy results, while all around us the other dancers were swirling and laughing, having a high old time. If you looked at the scene with the sound off, you would not notice anything unusual. But, in truth, the actress and I were the only ones making any noise at all. All the dancers were shuffling around the floor in their stocking feet—no shoes because of the noise—and though they were moving their mouths as if they were talking, they were not making any sound. The sounds of the crowd were added later. There was also no music to dance to, by the way. The director would play the music just long enough to get everybody moving around the floor and then would cut the music while the scene continued. Remember this story next time you see a dance scene in a movie and wonder why the dancers don't seem to have any rhythm. The likelihood is that they weren't hearing any music.

Walla performers use a lot of improvisational skills and are frequently very good with accents. In that bus station, for instance, it might be an advantage to hear a French woman and a Southern man, as well as perhaps some Mexicans.

Walla employment is centered mainly in Los Angeles and New York, where the bulk of movie and TV production happens. In L.A. there are approximately forty groups active in the field. There is no clear-cut route to the jobs. You'll have to talk to other actors, network in classes, find out who the walla producers are. Then get your voice demo tape to them. The work pays union scale as a rule, plus residuals for reuse. I personally know some folks making a very good living from this kind of work.

COMPUTER GAMES

This is the big growth area of the voice world these days. Whether played on Nintendo or Sony Play Stations or CD-ROMs, all computer games need voices. The demands on performers are similar to those in animated cartoons. You have to be able to do several distinct character voices in one sitting, and it helps if you can do accents. The lady who did the munchkin voices would be a natural.

GETTING STARTED

In order to get into the voice-over game, you need a demo tape that is tailored to the specialty you want to pursue. An animation tape sounds completely different from a more serious narration tape, and a commercial voice-over demo tape is yet another style. Whereas you can get a headshot photo taken for a couple of hundred dollars and start chasing casting directors and agents for on-camera work, voice work requires a professionally produced demo tape that can cost a lot more. I know one fellow who went through some classes and then had a tape produced, spending about $2,000. You can get away for half that if you can skip the classes. If you believe you already know what you are doing, you can go directly to the recording studio to make a demo with the assistance of an in-house studio producer.

But most newcomers do start in a class. In major markets, classes are taught by voice professionals and occasionally by casting directors who specialize in voices. Sometimes ad agency producers are brought in to give some pointers. Students learn voice-over skills while making contacts in the biz (i.e., potential employers). Classes are also a good place to hear competitive demo tapes of working pros.

The standard demo tape is no more than five minutes long. It should sound like copies of work that is "off the air," should contain sound effects and music, the whole nine yards. The casual listener should not be able to tell whether the work on the tape is a copy of actual paid employment or something you produced yourself. This is not the kind of thing you can do in your living room with car noises and parakeets in the background. You need to go into a recording studio with a professional producer to get the best results. Remember, when you start pursuing the work, you will be up against people who have highly competitive demo tapes. Success breeds success. There is no wading pool when it comes to voice-over work; if you want to do it, you have to swim with the big fish right from the start.

It is wise to spend a little extra and have your demo done on a DAT (digital audio tape) master, as opposed to the traditional reel-to-reel format. The reason for this is that some casting directors have computer setups in their offices now that allow them to put a DAT tape directly onto their hard drive. The casting director for one major company told me that, if he is looking for the voice of a crocodile for a computer game, he can just type in "crocodile voice" on his computer, and up will come half a dozen names he has predetermined can deliver such a creature. The performer's name, perhaps a photo, and a digitized demo tape (from that DAT master) are readily available on the computer. Click, click, click . . .

MARKETING YOURSELF

Once you have a demo tape in your hand, you try to get an agent to represent you. In L.A. and New York, there are agents who specialize exclusively in representing voice performers. In smaller markets, most talent agencies are "full service," representing performers for on-camera work as well as voices. Whatever your local situation is, you will need an agent if you want to be considered for the best auditions. Agents talk to producers and casting directors, and you want them to be talking about you.

You can also send your tape directly to potential employers. The employment scene is a bit like the Wild, Wild West, so you'll have to find your own way. Most major corporations in America have human resources departments, so that might be a good place to begin. Try to locate the people in the company who are in charge of making in-house educational films, employee training films, that kind of thing. Or at ad agencies, hit the producers and creative directors. Go to your library and see if they have a copy of the *Red Book*. Published by the AAAA (Advertising Agency Association of America), this telephone-book-sized volume lists all major ad agencies, broken down by the products they advertise, and tells who is who within the agency. Some performers send their demo tapes to ad agencies all over the United States.

You can also send your tape directly to casting directors at ad agencies and big software companies. Most of them listen to these regularly. One fellow told me he listens to tapes in his car as he drives to work. The point is that, though it is highly desirable that you have an agent to represent you, it is possible to get the ball rolling all by yourself if you have some hustle and a good demo tape. Then, after you have landed a few jobs, maybe those agents will be more interested.

WANT MORE INFO?

Check out *Word of Mouth: A Guide to Commercial Voice-Over Excellence* by Susan Blu and Molly Ann Mullin (Pomegranate Press, 1996) and *There's Money Where Your Mouth Is: An Insider's Guide to a Career in Voice-Overs* by Elaine A. Clark (Back Stage Books, 1995). Both of these are no-nonsense in-depth explorations of the subject written by pros in the field.

A SOBERING POSTSCRIPT

The voice world, at least as it applies to radio and TV commercials, is male dominated. More than 80 percent of the voices in commercials are male, in fact. Screen Actors Guild and AFTRA have been active in trying to correct this imbalance, but we struggle against preconceived notions on Madison Avenue that male voices are more trust-inspiring, that they "sell better." Progress is being made slowly, and the beat goes on.

CHAPTER 6

Auditioning
for TV Shows

Want some statistics? Try these on for size: Television consumes 600,000 hours of programming each year. An episode of a typical prime-time action-adventure is shot in about a week. Daytime soap operas are usually shot at the incredible rate of one episode a day.

We're talking about a Marx Brothers frenzy here. The producers of a TV hit could well be responsible for delivering twenty episodes of their show in just about as many weeks. The wonder is that this pace allows for any quality at all.

Though there is some TV production in cities across the United States, Hollywood remains the king of the mountain as a production center, and actors who live there have a competitive advantage. In the heat of the season, during the fall and winter, casting sessions are held all over town, usually in small production offices on the various studio lots. Disney, CBS Studio Center, Paramount, Universal, 20th Century-Fox, Warner Bros., and the Culver Studios are where a lot of the action takes place.

When a Hollywood-based show shoots on location out of town, local actors are usually hired for the smaller roles as a cost-cutting measure. It's usually cheaper to do that than it is to transport actors from southern California, complete with per diem and hotel bills. Auditions for these smaller roles might be held in the offices of a local talent agent or independent casting director, in makeshift production offices, or even a hotel room. Wherever they take place, the procedures are exactly the same as in Hollywood except that you are more likely to be put on videotape.

When I arrived on the West Coast in 1976, fresh from eight years on the New York stage and stock, I confess to being astonished at the way TV shows are cast. Shock number one was that actors in Hollywood have to audition for single-line roles. After all, what can you do with "They went that-a-way!" in an audition? Probably because stage plays rarely have roles that small, I had never focused on the possibility that actors might have to take script in hand, stand up in front of the folks, and give a single line their best shot.

Shock number two was this business of "sides." The first time my agent arranged a reading for me and said that I could "pick up the sides any time before the audition," I hustled right over there, walked onto the Paramount lot, waved at the guards, found the production office, introduced myself to the receptionist . . . and was given two pages out of a script. "You are reading for Man 2 at the bar," she told me as I quickly scanned the pages. Sure enough, there were two lines for Man 2, one on the first page and the one on the second. "Is there a complete script for this?" I asked. "No, the character is just in that one scene." "Oh." Again, with my stage background, I was ill-prepared for the way things are done in televisionland.

The likelihood is that you, too, will begin your Hollywood days with these little roles, so be prepared. The only exceptions are for actors who arrive with entree of some sort, people who manage to leapfrog to a higher rung on the ladder and get top-level representation. If you've recently had the lead in a Broadway play and got boffo reviews, you're in luck. Catch a plane.

HOW TV CASTING WORKS

Auditions for TV shows in Hollywood are conducted "live" about 97 percent of the time and are held in cramped production offices that have a living-room motif. Videotape is starting to find its way into the process, but it is so rarely used in Hollywood that it is almost not worth mentioning. The usual procedure is for the actor to read with a casting director in the presence of an assembled group of writers, producers, and the director. Unless the role is a major one, callbacks are nonexistent. You usually work within a week of that initial audition.

Unless you're working on a three-camera sitcom that will be shot in front of a live audience, you shouldn't anticipate any rehearsal time at all in TV. Actors are expected to have their lines committed to memory and to be ready to cook when they arrive on the set. Rehearsal consists of running over things with the director while the crew is setting up lights and camera. Frequently you don't even know who the director is until someone steps out of the crowd, introduces himself or herself, and walks you through the scene.

If you come from a stage background, this way of working can be extremely unnerving. You always have the feeling that you are going off half-cocked, giving performances that are, to be charitable, somewhat lacking in depth. There is zero opportunity for exploration of your character, so you have to go with the most obvious choices.

The reason for this is that frantic production pace I mentioned. Everybody is running to keep up in this business. The networks make their program purchases in late spring or early summer, usually the month of May, and that leaves producers only a matter of weeks to get into production since shows have to be ready for the start of the fall season. In an ideal world, they would love to rehearse and make nice art, but there simply isn't any time. The dynamic is more like a bunch of runners popping out of the starting gate.

This fact of television life has dramatic implications for the actor in the audition room. Because there isn't going to be any time for rehearsal, they want to see precisely what you plan to do when you show up on the set. In short, they want to see the performance.

Think about this now: in a commercial, you're only dealing with a thirty-second framework at most, and they are going to shoot that same thirty seconds over and over and over again until they get exactly what they want. Therefore, it isn't necessary to show *the* performance in audition. Your scene in a TV show, on the other hand, is likely only one of several that must be shot on the same day. You aren't going to get the chance to do it again and again. You'll get one take, maybe two, sometimes three, and they'll do enough angles to allow for editing choices. A master, a couple of close-ups, and then on to the next setup.

Television, therefore, puts a high premium on a fast-study, one-take actor, the kind of person who is willing to leap to performance, willing to do precisely the things that a good acting teacher will pin your ears for. I once heard someone describe acting on TV as "not acting at all, but rather something like acting," and I don't think he was far off the mark.

Auditions call for the strongest possible choices from actors,

73

and sometimes you can come out smelling like a rose with choices that have nothing to do with the character. I once went to a Broadway audition and performed Lucky's speech from *Waiting For Godot* backward, last word first, first word last. They loved it, and I got called back.

TV is another matter, and you have to tread carefully. Yes, make strong choices, but watch out that you don't make strange ones. I could never have gotten away with my backward *Waiting for Godot* inventiveness, for example. Whatever you do in the audition room should be within the realm of what you will do if you get hired. These guys do not want surprises. They are working under incredible pressure and want reassurance. They do not delight in the unknown, and they aren't looking forward to a rehearsal process in which we all get together and work it out. They want to know what you plan to do and, if they hire you, want you to do precisely that when you work.

THREE-CAMERA VS. EPISODIC PROGRAMS VS. SOAP OPERAS

A distinction should be made between three-camera sitcoms, typically videotaped in front of a live audience, and episodic programs that are shot on 35mm film on sound stages and location. In fairness, the former does have something resembling rehearsal, sort of like souped-up one-week summer stock. The cast is assembled on Monday, rehearses through the week, and tapes on Friday. They still want to see the performance at the audition, though, because a lot of the rehearsal has to do with making scenes work for camera and script rewrites. Soap operas operate on a production schedule of one show per day, so the concept of rehearsal there is almost amusing: you show up in the morning, go through it three or four times, make adjustments for script changes, and then tape in the afternoon. For soap opera auditions, they want the same thing—the performance.

THE CURSE OF SIDES

For the casting director, sides are a great convenience and cost-saving device. All he or she does is photocopy the specific pages in which each character appears and let the actors audition using those instead of an entire script. If the character appears in several different scenes scattered through the script, then all those scenes may be excerpted and stapled together.

For the actor, sides present a triple whammy. As any self-respecting stage actor knows, characters do not stand alone. They interrelate with other characters and with situations. Anybody who has ever studied with Uta Hagen or Stella Adler knows how to break down a script to come up with an intelligent analysis. We learn that it is something close to a mortal sin to pull a monologue out of context in a play and simply commit it to memory. Well, welcome to La La Land, the place where rules of convention are turned on their head.

This story will give you an idea of how awkward it can be to audition with sides. I was up for a nice role in a hit show produced by Universal. The character owned a jewelry store, and there was a robbery. Three scenes were involved. The first scene establishes the relationship between the owner and his assistant: this is a quality jewelry store, not a pawn shop. Suddenly, the robbers run in, two of them with guns drawn. "Everybody lie on the floor!" they order as they snatch jewels from shelves and stuff them in their bags. Without warning, one of the robbers turns at the door and shoots the prone assistant in the back, killing him instantly. They flee as burglar alarms scream. Scene number two has the star of the show talking quietly and sympathetically with the distraught store owner. Scene number three takes place several days later down at the police station: question and answer time. By this time, the owner is subdued and rather depressed, no longer hysterical.

In the audition, the casting director read all of the parts except mine, making it necessary for me to jump in when it was my turn. More important, however, she went directly from one scene to the next without a moment of transition. There was no way for me, with the owner's part, to make adjustments to incorporate all of the violence and mayhem. There I was, screaming, "You killed him!" at the robbers and then, spinning on a dime, I had to be immediately distraught in the scene with the hero. Spinning again, I had to mentally cut to two days later, flinging myself into a depressed reading. It was enough to give an actor nosebleed.

Was it a fair audition? Did the producers get an accurate idea of what I might do with the role? Not really, because on the actual job, though there wouldn't be time for rehearsal, I would have time to consider the transitions. The scenes might not even be shot on the same day. This audition was absolutely typical, however, and every other actor out there in the waiting room had to go through the same mess. I didn't get that particular role.

Why do they do that? Why put actors through a wringer audition? Simple. Just as they don't have any time to rehearse, they also don't have any time to cast. They have six or thirteen or twenty episodes to shoot, are already two weeks off-schedule because the star has the flu, or are just coming out of a strike. Casting is simply one more hassle to have to hurry up and deal with. From where the executives are sitting, an actor who has to be nursed along with such niceties as transition time and rehearsal probably won't be able to work at the pace demanded by TV anyway.

PREPARING FOR THE AUDITION

Check in with the receptionist when you arrive. If you haven't already received sides, the receptionist will give them to you. Sign in if you see any sign-in sheets lying around. Fewer actors are seen for these roles than are seen for commercials so you don't have to worry about being kept too long in the waiting room. It is rare that you will have to wait longer than thirty minutes before being called in.

Your audition will almost certainly involve a dialogue situation of some kind, and you'll be reading with the casting director, so there is not much to be gained by talking to light switches in preparation for it. Instead, you should spend your time considering clear, strong choices that will propel you into the reading and carry you through. Look for subtext, conflict, relationship, humor.

Personally, I like to get away from the other actors in the waiting room so that I'm not distracted. It's okay to tell the receptionist to come and get you out in the hallway when they are ready for you. Stay away from mirrors (unless you are laughing at yourself in them) for the same reasons I cited in the commercial section. You can't be the actor and the audience simultaneously.

Time will seem to fly in the audition room, so you want to do everything you can to gain control of the situation. If possible, pick up the sides in advance of the audition (or have your agent fax them to you) so you can see what kind of monster you are dealing with. Pay particular attention to the page numbers on the sides—that is the easiest way to tell if you are going to be reading multiple scenes. Use a hi-lighter or magic marker to underline your lines. Be bold with your markings (you won't have to return the sides); under the tension in the audition room the script can become a blur, and bold markings can be your personal road map. Be sure to mark transition points clearly so you can see them under pressure.

Create a context for each scene, even if you are not sure it is correct. Examine the relationship between the characters. Are they friends? Don't know? Could they be? Fine. They're friends, then. What time of day does the scene occur? Is the character tired or alert? If your character has a scene with the lead of the show, count your blessings and create the relationship. Is there any way in the world that the star and your character could know one another, be friends? If so, go for it. It's better to sin on the side of familiarity. Maybe it will give the writers the bright idea to put this "friend" back into another episode.

Give yourself a strong motivation for each scene, something that will really propel you. What does your character want in this scene? Or, put a better way, what do *I* want in this scene? (When working on a role, it is best to refer to your character in the first person right from the start. It breaks down the distance, helps you "own" it quickly.)

Use substitution if the scenes don't have a context that invites color and depth. In the jewelry store robbery, I pretended that the assistant who got killed was my real-life brother, Richard. The people watching the reading didn't know the difference, but the substitution gave me something stronger to react to when the robbers shot him. It also helped raise the stakes for the next scene, where I had to be so distraught.

If at all possible, be familiar with the format of the show. I make it a personal policy to watch at least one episode of every new show each season—no matter how awful they might be. It is best to have a "feel" for a show at the audition, and you can't always get that from the sides.

Look for ways your character can emotionally "turn corners" during the reading. I'm not talking about major transitions but subtle ones. If there is any way, for example, to have the character start the scene laughing and end the scene somber, do it.

THE AUDITIONING PROCESS

In TV auditions, the auditors are usually no more than a few feet from you. You'll read with the casting director, but the actual director will give you direction. You may go through it once or twice (usually just once), then it's all over. One advantage of having the auditors so close to you is that you can get a good sense of whether they like what you are doing. I recall one watershed audition at 20th Century-Fox. I read through the scene twice with the casting director as the assembled production team watched. It wasn't working. I knew the next words out of the director's mouth would be "thank you," but I also knew I didn't have the part, so I asked if I could try something wild and improvisational with the scene. They looked at one another, and the director said to go ahead. I then went way out on a limb, further than I normally would in a TV audition, and it worked. The character as written was extreme, a real mental case, and when I extended it, something clicked. Needless to say, I got the role, and to make matters even better, the producer of that show was Glen Larson, one of the busiest producers in Hollywood. He saw what I did that day, and ever since has simply hired me for his shows with no audition. I've now worked for him many times, and it all came from reading the faces in that audition room. Here are a few pointers:

- Remember to use humor. These pressure-cooker situations send humor flying right out the window. If you can find any way at all to justify it, smile, laugh, chuckle. Play opposites.
- When they offer you a chair, scoot it a few inches one way or the other. They've gotten used to seeing actor after actor in that chair. By moving it, you "own" it and are subtly taking charge of the room.
- Keep the script in your hand even if you have memorized the part. Refer to it from time to time. Even though there isn't going to be any rehearsal, the implication is that if you are this wonderful with a script in your hand, just imagine how extraordinary your performance will be once you have had time to get off script.
- When reading, make eye contact with the casting director as much as possible. Let the auditors see your reactions. Don't bury your head in the script.
- Try to control the pace of the scene. The casting director will probably read too fast, and you can usually break the rhythm when you are speaking. Look for ways to pause midsentence, to reflect, to shift your intention. If you control the pace, the auditors will hang on your every word. It is another way of "taking stage," or controlling the room. Remember, the producers and directors want you, the actor, to be in charge. Show them what you will do if you are cast in the role.

- Never, ever touch the casting director. I give this advice from personal experience as a casting director. Actors have a lot of adrenaline flowing in audition situations, and if they start grabbing the casting director, things can get rough. I have had my shirt torn and have emerged from casting sessions scratched and bruised by enthusiastic actors. The best policy is "hands off."

- Since the casting director is going to be reading all of the parts except yours, find ways to differentiate between the characters. The casting director is likely to deliver the lines of the robbers pretty much like the lines of the cops, but you should know how to relate to the cops and robbers in different ways.

- Controlling the pace of the scene is a good thing to do, but in general good actors want to take *too* many dramatic pauses. Therefore, unless you are purposely trying to break the pace set by the casting director, use this device sparingly. In life we tend to perk along, and that will ring truest in a reading.

- Feel free to get up and move around if you want. The chair is there for your convenience. Be careful, though, that you don't get caught up in aimless pacing. Also, remember that these audition rooms are usually quite small and cramped. There isn't much place to travel. If a scene calls for your character to enter the room, you might want to stand at the office door and, as you begin, turn to face the group. That will give you the option of doing the scene standing or sitting.

Acting is about *doing* something, right? We learn in acting classes that acting has very little to do with words. You know it, and I know it, but for some reason, many people who write for TV apparently don't. They tend to put in too much expository talking and ho-hum filler. Many of the supporting roles that you will audition for seem to exist for no other reason than to provide the lead of the show with some tidbit of information. For example, the need will arise to somehow communicate to the lead the news that the prime suspect has moved out of his apartment. Easy— let's just invent a cleaning woman and let her tell him about it. The actor comes into the audition and finds two pages of pure exposition to render. Lots of names, addresses, and times—dull, dull, dull. An old salt told me once that, when it comes to television, "The producers provide the lines, and the actor provides the character." Sounds right to me.

The trick is to bring an attitude to such roles, a context, a reason for living that is not in the script. Maybe this is the fourth time this week that the cleaning woman has had to answer questions about this particular tenant, and she's getting darned tired of it. Or maybe the cleaning woman thinks this particular cop is cute. Or maybe he reminds her of her own son. Maybe she harbors a secret desire to be a detective herself, so when she starts telling about the suspect moving out, she does so with a conspiratorial tone. Get it? Try to find some place to hang your hat with a character.

Now, a special comment about those one- and two-line roles, the kind you audition for with a single sheet of paper. They pay the bills and at the beginning you are going to do them. Remember this, however: The show is not about the fellow who yells, "They went that-a-way!" Don't overdo it in the audition room. Don't try to make it into something that it's not because you'll just scare the producers. If you were up for the role of a waitress, for example, and your only line was "Be with you in a minute, Sir," you wouldn't want to deliver it as if you and the star of the show had had a lover's quarrel and you are avoiding him now. You wouldn't want to stare daggers at him. Just get busy with your waitressing, justify your choices in terms of restaurant activity, and do your job.

PILOTS, EPISODICS, AND MADE-FOR-TV MOVIES

The workaday money for actors in Hollywood comes from episodic TV shows and sitcoms (and commercials, of course). They are great because you get paid to do the show, and then you get paid 100 percent of that when it reruns again in the summer. And you get paid when the show goes into syndication. And you get paid again when it is sold overseas, though by this point your checks are down to about $8.46 per episode. Virtually everybody is anxious to work on the hit shows for this payment schedule. If you build up a resume of work on successful episodics and sitcoms, the residuals will arrive in the mail for many years. I still receive small checks for work I did fifteen years ago!

Pilot season is the Kentucky Derby of the television industry. It stretches from late winter to spring, during which time production companies turn out sample episodes of prospective TV series. These sample episodes are picked over by the networks, and a few receive orders for additional episodes and are assigned a slot in the fall schedule. Most of those that get on the air will fail to draw a big enough audience and will be cancelled. But a few—a precious few—will succeed. If you are fortunate enough to have a regular role on a hit TV series (about the same odds as hitting the lottery), you can start collecting $10,000-plus per episode and answering fan mail.

A casting director who announces casting for a pilot is literally flooded with photos and resumes—thousands of them—from both coasts, from agents everywhere, and from actors and their managers. The casting director sorts through the deluge, holds private auditions and meetings to prescreen the most likely candidates, and then decides who gets to read for the producers.

The starring roles in pilots generally go to a pool of actors who are already known in the industry. Frequently, they don't have to audition during prescreens. Instead, they "take meetings" with the casting director, and their agents send their demo reels around for the execs to check out. Maybe they audition at the final callbacks. It's a different ball game, one we all want to play in. If actors in this group do have to endure auditions, they are generally treated with more respect than "day players," who are hired on a per-show basis. They are given complete scripts in advance and alloted ample audition time. It's sort of like the difference between flying first class and tourist.

If you have the good fortune to land an audition for a strong role in a pilot, and if the producers were to like you, it is likely that you will have to read several times—a couple of times for the producers and writers and then again for the stone-faced network execs, affectionately known as "the suits." You might even have to go through a screen test. It can be a unique form of prolonged and excruciating torture, knowing that stardom could be just a whisper away. After casting is narrowed down to a few final candidates, negotiations are held with each actor's agent just in case he or she is chosen. Contracts are signed for a series deal, contingent upon final casting, a deal that specifies how much the actor will be paid in the first season, the second season, and so on. That way, a performer who is chosen for a good role can't turn around at the audition door and say to the producers, "Want me, huh? Well it's going to cost you $18 million!" The contracts have already been signed, sealed, and delivered.

Made-for-TV movies are like little feel-good feature films with spaces for commercials, and auditioning for them is just like going up for an episodic. The average budget is a bit over $4 million, compared to the $20 million-plus for feature films, and they take about twenty days to shoot. Many of them are barely disguised trial balloons for possible series.

BILLING

This is one of the really silly facets of television. Billing is a negotiable item. Theoretically, a *featured* role is the smallest kind you can play, *costar* is the next step up, and *guest star* is the highest rung on the ladder short of being a regular on the show. You would think that the size of the part has a mathematical and inflexible relationship to the billing on the screen—that someone billed as a costar is playing a true lead. In Hollywood, there is no such logic. The way the game is played is this: when you are hired to play a role, your agent has to negotiate both money and billing with the casting director, who operates within parameters already set by the show's producers. In the case of large roles, true guest-star parts, the whole thing is easy. Billing is guest-star billing, and money is "top of the show."

With the smaller supporting roles, the box starts losing its shape. Whatever you got paid on your last job is your "rate" or "quote," and the unspoken law of the jungle is that the present employer is going to pay at least the same. When you hear actors say, "They're paying my rate," that's what they mean.

But suppose you got paid $1,000 a day on your last job and got costar billing; and suppose that the present job isn't as big as the last one you did and isn't worth $1,000 a day. Suppose the casting director is offering $800 a day and featured billing. Your agent might respond by saying, "Well, she really wants to do this show, so we'll take the $800 on a 'no-quote' basis, but we have to have costar billing." If the casting director agrees, what they are saying is that the current show will pay less than your rate, but nobody will tell, so the higher amount you got on your previous job remains your quote. Isn't this wonderful? Stanislavsky would be turning over in his grave.

It is possible to negotiate better billing than a role is in fact worth, particularly if the money is not there. Once you crack the guest-star barrier, however, it would be something close to a mortal sin to work in a featured part, a testament to your failing career. Oh, you might fudge and accept a costar role, but never a featured one. Even if you were doing a favor for the producer of the show by accepting a two-line part, you could not accept featured billing because you officially work at the guest-star level. Mind you, none of this is actually written down anywhere. It is just common knowledge in the biz.

Another negotiable item is *where* your billing appears. The best place is in the opening credits because viewers are theoretically paying more attention then. And it is highly desirable to have a "separate card," meaning that your name appears on screen by itself. If you don't negotiate a separate card, then your name will appear on a "shared card" with other actors' names. Perish the thought. Featured billing invariably appears in the end credits, as does costar most of the time. Opening credits are usually reserved for star billing, major guest stars, and regulars.

The least desirable billing, the absolute bottom of the barrel, is "end credits at producer's discretion." That means your name may or may not show up at all and, if it does, it will surely be buried in the end credits that go by so fast no one except you and your mom will notice.

There are variables on all of this, but you get the idea. The bubble I want to burst here is the idea that there is a correlation between the size of the part and billing on TV. It's all highly negotiable.

THE FUTURE OF TELEVISION

As a source of employment for actors, television programs and the commercials they deliver will continue to dominate. Currently, SAG members earn upward of $700 million from commercials each year plus an additional $350 million from the shows themselves. Combined, this income is two to three times as much as actors earn from movies. As long as the United States is a consumer society, and as long as television is a prime vehicle for delivering consumers to the advertising messages, television will dominate as an income source for actors.

The shape of television is changing as analog recording and transmission gives way to digital, but this will only enhance the medium as an income source. Network viewership for the Big Three networks—NBC, CBS, and ABC—has dropped below 50 percent, and cable viewership has soared. As discussed in Chapter 14 of this book, this development is a prime factor in the longest SAG strike in history. Because there is growing intergration and cross-fertilization between television and the Internet, and because audiences are expanding globally, it is increasingly difficult to monitor per-use formulas of actor compensation. Digital duplication makes it easy to send programs and commercials into cyberspace, where they can be downloaded and copied, and audience size is going to be increasingly difficult to measure. When the average computer user has high-speed access to the Internet via DSL and ISDN lines, advertisers will begin placing live-action commercials on both television and the Internet. Right now, the majority of Internet ads are of the banner variety, which are really more similar to print advertising than television commercials, but this is bound to change. The telephone companies across America are already backlogged with orders for high-speed lines. Due to consumer demand, in large markets it can take months to get the service installed. The important point for actors to remember is that the technology already exists. The cost of computers and the Internet is now within reason for the average consumer, and advertisers have a strong financial incentive to take advantage of that fact. That is why television and computers are merging, and that is why television will continue to dominate as an income source for actors.

Gazing into the media crystal ball is a popular activity, and various scenarios for the future are being tossed about by industry experts. All of them predict the eventual merger of television, computers, and telephone companies, and all of them see a vast expansion in the Internet. In the future, people will use their televisions not only to watch their favorite programs, but also for shopping, banking, investments, and keeping up with their children's school activities. I'm reminded of the wonderful phrase by the great southern writer Flannery O'Connor: "Everything that rises must converge." And so it is with the world of television and computers. We're just around the corner from having programming-on-demand displayed on multifunction, high-definition digital television sets. It would be an understatement to proclaim that television as we have known it is losing its shape. This is probably the most exciting time for television since its founding in the 1940s.

Commercially sponsored network television seems to be evolving along the lines of the Broadway theater, chasing the largest possible audiences, presenting lowest-common-denominator fare, aimed primarily at the free-spending eighteen- to forty-nine-year-old market. If a prime-time show attracts an audience of only five or six million viewers, it is considered a failure. More challenging material, as well as programming designed for viewers over fifty years old and children, is being siphoned off to subscriber-supported cable outlets such as HBO, Nickelodeon, Bravo, and A&E, which can profitably produce shows for smaller audiences. And, for the moment at least, we still have PBS, which has a history of producing quality programming.

If anything, there will be increased employment for actors in this hydra-headed television world of the future. Pay rates may decline as more programs are produced for smaller audiences, but there should be a greater volume of work, more chances to practice your craft.

CHAPTER 7

Auditioning for Movies

Is there really such a creature as a "film actor" as opposed to a "stage actor" or "TV actor"? Before I moved to the West Coast, I harbored the romantic notion of the actor as a traveling player and would have dismissed this question out of hand. Art was what it was all about and that began and ended right under the proscenium arch. From my perspective, movies were about commerce, klieg lights, moguls, palm trees, anything but art. Sure, you had your occasional *On the Waterfront* or *Rebel Without a Cause*, but essentially movies equaled Hollywood, and Hollywood equaled Mickey Rooney. Television, by my reckoning, was only good for the income to be earned from commercials, which was something you did to keep food on the table so you could keep doing plays. Now, after spending twenty years immersed in a world of Neilsen Ratings and screenings instead of New York opening nights, I can't be quite so smug. I still cling to the belief that acting is an art form, but I've learned that the art is in the person, not in the media. Working actors regularly shift back and forth between TV, film, and stage with no accompanying loss of integrity. The interesting thing is how some performers seem to glow on film while others seem to be ideally suited to TV or stage. Why is that? Could it be that there really is something called a "film actor"? And why do some actors become movie stars while others get their own series?

Walter Kerr wrote a marvelous article some years back in the *New York Times* in which he observed that a "larger than life" quality seems to be inherent in many stage stars. He cited Carol Channing as someone who, if you met her on the street, would appear to be an amalgamation of disparate features: a very large mouth, extremely big eyes, a voice of unusual distinction. But on stage, all of that blends into a whole that perfectly bridges the gap between actor and audience. I think he was on to something. Though he didn't say so, Miss Channing is an uncomfortable fit on the big screen; the very factors that serve as her assets on stage are liabilities when everything is amplified mechanically. In fact, some of the finest actors in this country simply don't translate well to film.

Why is it that James Dean was such a natural movie actor? Why John Wayne and Joan Crawford? Ted Danson and Bill Cosby swing back and forth between TV and movies and sell lots of tickets with their names over the title, but you somehow get the idea that even though they have successfully capitalized on TV fame in order to work in features, they are still essentially TV people. Goldie Hawn, on the other hand, easily made the leap from television to film. Irene Worth, Uta Hagen, and Joel Grey rarely venture far from the New York legitimate theater, where their name on the marquee virtually assures a hit.

What's the variable? Lord knows it is not a matter of raw talent. If it were, then Angela Lansbury and Hal Linden, among many others, would be known as movie stars rather than stage or TV stars. And it isn't merely a matter of where a performer gets his first break. Clint Eastwood first worked on TV, but there is no question he is a top-of-the-pile movie star. Same with the late Steve McQueen. Some argue that, when TV stars venture into film, it helps their chances of crossing over if they are expanding on the already existing persona they have developed on the tube. Michael J. Fox, for example, successfully made the leap from TV to film with *Back to the Future,* but he misstepped badly right after that when he starred in the dramatic film *Casualties of War.* His work in this latter movie was fine, but the role did not fit the public's perception of him. He's a sitcom kind of guy.

Movies and stage have something in common that television doesn't share, and that may be the key to the puzzle: neither answers directly to Madison Avenue. As we have already discussed, a nonthreatening sense of life is a critical ingredient for people who act in commercials and, since TV as a medium pretty much exists to deliver good-humored consumers to the advertisers, maybe that same dynamic is essential to actors who work on TV in general. Movies and stage, by contrast, answer only to the ticket purchaser and, though they aim to entertain, don't necessarily have to keep the audience in a mood to buy Wheaties or

Comet. If you think about it, most major movie stars exude an air of unpredictability, even danger. Think of Robert DeNiro, Nicholas Cage, Barbra Streisand, Al Pacino, Dustin Hoffman, Jack Nicholson, Marlon Brando, Meryl Streep, Glenn Close, James Woods, Michelle Pfeiffer—all of whom have strong, indelible personalities. When they make their rare appearances on TV, they are out of their element, too hot to handle in a manner of speaking. They carry enough voltage to blow out the fuse box. Remember the character JR, played by Larry Hagman, on the long-running television show *Dallas*? He was a TV villain, not a real villain. A real villain was played by Anthony Hopkins in the film *Silence of the Lambs*. Hagman, regardless of how nasty he behaved, left the viewer in a mood to sashay over to the neighborhood Burger King. Hopkins left the viewer in a mood not to leave the house without a weapon.

In a conversation I had with a major movie casting director in Hollywood, we discussed this question about movie actors versus TV actors. She observed that she could tell in a first meeting if an actor will work best on TV or movies. How? She didn't know. A hunch, maybe, a sense that a particular actor has an off-center quality or look that will work well on the big screen.

What I've finally come around to is this: Yes, there is such a thing as a film actor if by that you mean someone whose appearance and personality synthesize perfectly in movies in a way that they don't on stage or TV. Some actors literally go through an ugly duck–lovely swan transformation in the medium and become stars. By the same token, there are actors who seem incomplete unless they are standing on the legitimate stage. Like Ian McKellen or the late Laurence Olivier, when they make their entrance, the lights seem to get brighter. They belong there. However, all of this is absolutely beyond the actor's control, so you might as well just concentrate on the work. No matter how much film technique you develop, how skilled you become at working with the camera, film will either enhance you or it won't. If it doesn't, it isn't the end of the world because you can still act in movies, and can still play major leads in them. It only means that you aren't likely to be catapulted into the ranks of actors who are paid millions of dollars for making movies. The movies will be a place you visit rather than a place you live. Farrah Fawcett may star in movies, but she is not a movie star; Marilyn Monroe was a movie star.

As for whether or not you might be a "TV actor," it comes down to that nonthreatening, likable sense of life; again, there isn't much you can do about it. Because television literally broadcasts into the homes of forty million people at one time, and because advertisers are paying for the whole transaction, there is definitely a premium put on performers who are not going to overly stimulate, offend, or otherwise alienate consumers. Some top-notch television stars may not be the best actors in the world, but they draw multimillions in salary because the audiences like them. They successfully deliver the consumers to the commercials.

HOW MOVIES ARE CAST

The best way to get a handle on movie casting is to contrast the medium to TV. Consider budgets, for example: the average studio-produced feature film now costs about $50 million, and the average independent feature about $20 million. Compare these figures to the following TV costs: a one-hour segment of a prime-time episodic is about $1.2 million; a movie-of-the-week, about $2.5 million; a half-hour sitcom is in the $400,000 range; a game show, maybe $30,000; one episode of a soap opera, around $75,000.

What this means is that, in the movies, you have an awful lot of money being used to produce an hour and a half of images on celluloid. That in itself doesn't guarantee excellence, but it does assure a lot of attention to detail, starting with scripts and ending with casting, and it marks a striking difference between TV and movies. As we've already seen, television operates on a frantic agenda. A two-hour TV movie might be shot on a twenty-day schedule, but a feature film that length could easily take four months or longer. Movie makers tend to craft their film lovingly, turning out a one-of-a-kind work of art.

And then there is the element of magic, that intangible that makes movies a heart stopper for most actors. Movies are a more exotic form than TV, and this fact of life colors the entire production procedure. To a fly on the wall, a casting session for a movie looks identical to one for a TV show, but there are differences— hard to define, perhaps, but there nonetheless.

The casting director for a movie has a much closer relationship with the director than does his or her counterpart on TV. Directors come and go on television shows; typically they are hired for two or three episodes, while the show itself lives on. The casting director is part of the production team that is in place before a director is hired, and works more for the show than the director. Indeed, the casting director might not even be certain who the director is for next week's episode when he or she begins prescreening and preparing cast lists.

A movie casting director is hired for a single project and, before seeing the first actor, will have long talks with the director to discuss tone, style, maybe even the director's working methods. When I was casting the film version of Nathaniel West's book *Miss Lonelyhearts,* the director insisted that I bring in actors who projected a certain "emptiness." He wanted to capture the grays of the Depression era in Los Angeles, envisioning a movie full of long shadows, dusks, and lonely dawns; the actors had to fit, even those in the smallest roles. By the time I started prescreening, I was really an extension of the director's inner vision.

The closest equivalent in television to this kind of care would be in made-for-TV movies, but the budget doesn't allow for a lot of preproduction time and, anyway, directors and casting directors are bound by such considerations as TV Q , the quasi-secret coding system that measures actors' popularity with the TV audience. It is not unusual for a director of a TV movie to be given a list of "approved" actors from which to select the leads.

Next to arranging financing for the project and signing up stars, the most important decision a movie producer has to make is the hiring of the director. Once the director comes on board, he or she is the leader, and the production is tailored to his or her specifications. The director usually brings along an immediate production staff, including an assistant director and cinematographer, and frequently chooses the casting director. Compared to television, in which the director rides along with the production, in a movie, the director *is* the ride. The director's vision is the one that is expected to be up on the screen.

I'm not naive. I realize that some megastars have more power than most religious leaders and that, on their movies, everything is put together to fit their tastes. Such a star might well have final say on all casting, might even have the "final cut" in editing, and is likely to have a hand in hiring the director, too. There are, however, only a very few of these creatures, surely less than ten in the whole industry, and we do not need to include them or their projects in this discussion.

If you can compare the producer's optioning of a script or a novel to selecting a song, then hiring the director is like employing someone who will both arrange the song and select the musicians and singers. What the director wants filters down through the ranks in a very specific way, and this extends right into the casting sessions.

The mechanics of the movie casting session are identical to TV. The actors read from sides (as opposed to complete scripts) with the casting director in front of a group that certainly includes the director and may include producers and a writer, though screenwriters have less to do with casting than TV writers do. Usually, once a producer has optioned a script, the writer is out of the picture. Unless the audition is being held outside of Hollywood, videotape is seldom used, and screen tests may be required for major leads.

ACTING IN MOVIES

What is required for the screen actor, besides an essential 'animal' magnetism, is whatever's necessary to provide for the camera a true piece of experience. Whereas you can—and many effective actors do—get away with faking, posturing, and indicating emotions on stage, it's difficult if not impossible to get away with anything false before the camera. That instrument penetrates the husk of an actor; it reveals what's truly happening—if anything, if nothing. A close-up demands absolute truth; it's a severe and awesome trial. Acting for the screen is a more honest trade.

—Elia Kazan, director of *On the Waterfront*,
from his autobiography, *A Life*

In the beginning, there was the stage. The actor and the audience got together in the same place at the same time, and the actor had the responsibility of making sure that every member of the audience could see and hear what was going on. Given that a person sitting more than halfway back in an amphitheater might not be able to pick up the subtle shifts in an actor's eyes or the twitch of a mouth, the actor had to adjust to compensate for the distance.

Then came movies, a medium in which the actor's performance is carried to the audience through mechanical means—and at the discretion of the director and editor. No longer concerned with compensating for distance, actors found their performances extraordinarily amplified on the screen. A lifted eyebrow becomes a major event in extreme close-up when your face is twenty feet tall. That's why the wisdom in movies is that, when shooting close-ups, "if you think something, it is done." You don't need to "do" as much as you do on stage. Yes, you need to play your action, do all the things a good performance on stage would demand, but you don't need to take it to the audience in the same way. For someone from a stage background, this is a real adjustment to make. It is hard to trust the camera at first, to make it your partner, and you always have the feeling that you aren't doing enough.

You may have heard it said that "acting is reacting." Though this may be a generally useful perspective, on film it is really imperative. In the legitimate theater, the audience tends to watch the character who is talking; in movies, their attention is directed to the person who is listening. The next time you watch a movie, notice how they cut to reaction shots. For example, you may see a child dart into the street chasing a ball. Then, a quick cut to an extreme close-up of a woman driving a car. We see her react to the child, slamming on the brakes, horrified. Or, say a beautiful woman enters the room at a party, pausing at the door. The director may well cut to a reaction shot of a very interested man. We know immediately what he thinks of the woman, whether he knows her or not, whether he admires her beauty. Reaction, reaction, reaction. Yes, acting is "doing," but in the movies, you do less and react more.

I saw a graphic example of this while teaching a series of summer workshops on acting for camera. The purpose of the classes was to explore the differences between acting for stage versus acting for film, and the participants were, for the most part, highly experienced stage actors. Sprinkled among them were a few newcomers. Scenes were assigned, rehearsed, and then videotaped, complete with master shots, reverses, the works. Then we studied the results. Surprisingly, the new people frequently came off better than some of the old pros. Why? At first we were mystified by it but then, in a flash, it came clear: the new people didn't have enough craft yet to know about propelling a scene along! They only knew to stay in the present moment and to react. The experienced actors would aggressively pursue their objectives and, if teamed with less experienced actors, would try to compensate for what they perceived the newcomers were not doing. On stage they would have gotten away with it but on film they appeared uncentered, their concentration splintered. They seemed to be flailing.

Now, let me hasten to add that reacting rather than acting is decidedly not synonymous with having no energy. I have seen actors so concerned about doing too much for film that they managed to project a repressed dynamic. Movie acting does not equate to "small" or "quiet" or "low key." You don't want to come across as energyless or, worse, boring. Movies are not grim, and directors love actors with a good sense of humor and energy. Ideally, the scenes in a film depict the most important moments, not the most mundane. Theatrical reality is heightened reality, enriched. Audiences do not want to see just any old love affair. They want Romeo and Juliet. They don't want a garden-variety murder; they want to see *Silence of the Lambs*.

HELPFUL HINTS

Here are some special tips for auditioning for movies:

- You can presume the casting director is intimately familiar with the roles in the script and has a predetermined idea of what the director wants. Ask questions at a prescreen audition if you want to. Deal with the casting director of a movie in the same fashion you might if you were talking to the actual director.

- If you are naturally animated (as I am), remember to calm down a bit for film. Jumpy, jerky, helter-skelter movement might work great on stage, but on film it is a killer. Internalize. Same passion, just internalized. Yul Brynner once advised a new actor to "practice stillness." Good advice.

- Movie directors are influenced by an actor's personality and will likely take the time to chat with you. Be honest, not defensive. They are just trying to get to know you. Remember, the camera sees everything.

- By all means, show the director the actual performance. There may be a limited rehearsal period for the leads of the film, but supporting players are expected to show up on the set ready to cook, just like in TV. The difference is that, in movies, the director has the luxury of doing more takes than TV. Not as much pressure as a rule.

- If you have a theatrical "reel," take it with you to movie auditions. TV directors are usually too rushed to look at them, but an interested movie director just might. It could be the deciding factor needed to toss a role into your corner.

THE FUTURE OF MOVIES

As explained in Chapter 14, the big story of the day when it comes to movie production is the evolution of digital video. The financial success of *Blair Witch Project* inspired just about every Hollywood producer to start lining up digital projects. Even George Lucas is shooting the live-action segments of the next *Star Wars* movie on digital. Entertainment-industry trade papers are thick with reports of multiple digital picture deals, and the typical budget is in the $500,000 to $1 million range. Instead of producing one movie that costs $20 million, many producers are breaking up their overall production budgets into smaller digital packages.

When movies are shot digitally, they can be transferred to 35mm film for conventional exhibition in multiplexes or, since the visual images are already converted to zeros and ones, the language of computers, they can be uploaded into the Internet. The bottleneck in Internet exhibition is not on the production side, but on the bandwidth side. Computer users definitely need high-speed access in order to view live-action movies on their computers. Also, producers are still struggling with ways to limit unauthorized copying of digital movies. Despite the challenges, Jack Valenti, president of the Motion Picture Association of America, predicted that mainstream feature-length motion pictures will be available for downloading in as little as a year (*Daily Variety*, September 6, 2000). Keep an eye, too, on Internet "cyberplexes" such as Atom Films (www.atomfilms.com) and iFilm (www.iFilm.com). Already, you can download and watch more than 1,400 short live-action and animated movies from the iFilm web site, and new cyberplexes are appearing all the time. In time, digital downloading of movies from the Internet will undoubtedly replace VHS rentals altogether.

Foreign films and low-budget independent films shot traditionally on 35mm will continue to find a loyal market. Movies such as *All About My Mother* and *Run Lola Run*, both released by Sony Pictures Classics and both with budgets under $10 million, successfully played the art houses, along with U.S. independents such as David Mamet's *The Spanish Prisoner*. There will be a drift toward digital production of these movies, followed by Internet exhibition, but especially in urban areas, the art house crowd will remain for the foreseeable future.

INTERACTIVE MEDIA

Life was easier when we had only television shows, radio shows, and movies. Now we have multimedia, which covers everything from computer games to interactive television.

The 1994 AFTRA Interactive Media Agreement—the first performers' union attempt to cover the field—explained it this way:

> Interactive Media means any media (i.e., hardware) on which Interactive Programs operate and through which the user may interact with such Interactive Programs, including but not limited to personal computers, games, machines, arcade games, all CD-Interactive machines and any and all analogous, similar or dissimilar microprocessor-based units and the digitized, electronic or any other formats now known or hereinafter invented which may be utilized in connection therewith.

Doesn't help much, does it?

The confusion comes with that word *platform*. CD-ROM is a platform. Nintendo is a platform. Sony Play Station is a platform. The Internet is a platform. So when we refer to multimedia, we are really talking about platforms. The computer games are all similar in that they are interactive, but the platforms on which they may be played are different. It's multimedia if you play it next to the ice dispenser at the 7-Eleven, and it's multimedia if you play it on your home computer from a CD-ROM.

Income for professional actors is already into the millions of dollars each year from this source, even without reuse fees such as are common in commercials and TV shows. As it stands now, you do a day's work on a computer game, and you are paid for that day. The rate is $500 to $600 per day. No residuals, even if forty million people wind up playing the game. Surely this pay arrangement will be adjusted to include residuals when it becomes clear precisely how computer games are reused. The challenge is in the tracking. When a commercial or TV show is aired, a record is kept for each showing, and so residuals can be computed. Nobody knows for sure what happens with the games. Now that a growing number of them are being downloaded from the Internet, it should be easier to keep up with them, and actors' revenues from this source should increase.

BLUE-SCREEN ACTING

Computer games present special acting challenges. The performer typically acts in a specially prepared room that is completely blue. Blue background, blue foreground, blue walls. No sets, very few props. The actor must react and interact with things that are not, in reality, happening. A slimy outer space monster, for instance, sneaks onto the spaceship and our hero has to shoot it with his magic ray gun. In production, the actor has to stand on a mark on the floor and interact with the monster, shooting into thin air. Off to the side, the producer and director are watching the action on a computer screen and editing in the animated monster, bringing actor and monster together in the same picture. If the actor doesn't hit his marks precisely, he might suddenly disappear from the screen.

This is called "blue screen acting" and it is something we will all probably learn how to do before long. Actors who have experience in the field invariably report the weirdness of acting against blue walls and thin air. Everything is in the imagination, and improvisational ability is a definite plus. And it doesn't help anything that most of the directors are computer experts and not actor-oriented directors from a theatrical background. Therefore, they will likely give you "result" direction. Remember that term from the chapter on commercials?

Yet another acting challenge in this new field is caused by the fact that the typical script for a computer game is over five hundred pages long. Contrast that to the typical movie script, which is around 130 pages. I heard of one game script that ran to three thousand pages! The reason for this is the interactivity. The game player is really a character in the story, deciding which way to go, which way to react to the space monsters. The actors have to play all of the different variations. For instance, that fellow with the ray gun in his hand may shout "Take that!" at the space monster and fire away, killing the thing. That's Take One. On Take Two, the actor fires the gun—but it malfunctions, and the monster advances on him. On Take Three, he can't find his ray gun at all and runs from the room. The game player chooses the action, the actor plays the variations, hence thousands of pages of script.

CHAPTER 8

Auditioning for Multimedia/ Interactive Roles

Auditions for on-camera performers for computer games are videotaped, the same way as are those for commercials, and they are usually conducted by freelance casting directors. The big difference between these auditions and those for commercials or TV shows is that computer game scripts typically have multiple plot lines, known in the game biz as "branching." When you arrive at an audition for a computer game, you may have to puzzle over a script that requires you to do the same thing four times, with slight variations. And once you are in front of the camera, you may be required to go through some blue-screen-style acting, fighting off imaginary monsters.

INDUSTRIAL/EDUCATIONAL PRODUCTION

Clearly, computer games are not the only things that are interactive. Most major corporations in America now produce training videos that can be viewed on various platforms, including CD-ROMs. A new employee sits down at the computer, pops a CD-ROM in the drive, and is taught one-on-one how to operate a fork lift or repair a circuit board. Studies have shown that employees who are trained interactively have 50 percent higher retention than those who merely sit and listen to a lecture or watch a conventional training video.

Whether delivered on CD-ROM or in a standard videotape format, corporate training and informational videos present a unique challenge for the actor. Since these tapes won't be seen by the general public and are tailor-made for specific industries, they tend to be full of cryptic corporate jargon, the kind of stuff the average actor cannot be expected to know. Reading for them reminds me of exercises I used to do in acting class involving the "Jabberwocky" poem from Lewis Carroll's *Through the Looking Glass*. The idea was to act out various everyday scenarios—buying the groceries, getting the car fixed, and the like—while speaking only the Jabberwocky nonsense words. I have acted in corporate films in which I understood no more than 30 percent of what I was saying, but I had to make it seem as though I understood it all. The following sample script will illustrate the challenge:

FADE IN to discover BOB and CARL in a conference room. They are bent over some papers spread on the coffee table in front of them.

BOB

I really appreciate you taking this time with me, Carl. This DDAT proposal is the biggest project I've handled, and you are an expert in this area.

CARL

That's all right, Bob. Happy to help. You already have the basics, and if I can go over the format revisions with you, I think you'll come out smelling like a rose. Let's start with Phase I, okay?

BOB

Great! That's my biggest problem.

CARL

No sweat. You worked on the Pre-Allocation System, didn't you?

BOB

Sure. We all did.

CARL

Right. Well, Phase I actually came from the things we learned on that job. . . .

BOB

You mean, this is an extension of the Random Walk work that Lois and the fellows at BALCOM were doing?

CARL

Exactly. Let's take this first set of figures because they come directly from the PAS job.

You see the problem? This type of material presupposes all manner of knowledge that an actor can't be expected to have. What on earth is a "Pre-Allocation System," anyway? Is "DDAT" a kind of bug spray? The people who are going to watch the film know what all that means, so the actors have to pretend they do, too. And unlike the situation with strange commercial copy, you can't ask for quick explanations at the audition. You just have to wing it.

FINDING THE WORK

When a company wants to produce a training video, it will usually contract with an independent production house and/or director to get it done. The director, in turn, will arrange for casting. To save money, he or she might contact local talent agencies and ask to see actors on their premises, or—if there is a little extra to spend—might hire a freelance casting director who will call a lot of talent agents and have actors from all over town audition in a central casting studio, or might simply hire actors with whom he or she has worked in the past.

So the actor who wants to work in corporate videos has to be a bit of a trailblazer. Since very few corporations maintain casting files with 8x10 photos, you have to beat the bushes to find the jobs. It helps to have a talent agent who traffics in corporate videos. In Los Angeles, agents who specialize in commercials are more apt to get calls for corporate videos than are agents who specialize in movies and TV shows. In smaller markets, where talent agencies are "full service," representing actors for any and all paying jobs, corporate training films will be included in the mix.

Even if you do not have an agent, however, it is still possible to grab some of the fruit from this tree. A good place to start would be with a list of corporations with headquarters in your city. Get on the phone and ask for the human resources department, or the education or training department. Once connected, identify yourself as an actor and ask if they produce training films or videos for company use. If they do, ask if they maintain photo files. Ask if they work with any particular directors a lot. Try to get names you can track down. Then call the directors and ask if *they* maintain files.

Another good reference is one of the sourcebooks that are regularly used by the advertising industry. On the West Coast, the *411 Directory* is good, or the *REEL Directory* in San Francisco. In New York *The Madison Avenue Handbook* fills the same need. Since ad agencies use them, directors in search of work tend to advertise in them. Go down the list of directors and look for those claiming a specialty in educational/industrial/corporate films. Call them, following up with a photo in the mail and maybe a visit.

As mentioned earlier, some corporate films—particularly those being produced outside Los Angeles and New York—are cast in the offices of franchised talent agents who organize casting sessions for their own clients. If you don't happen to be represented by that agent, you will not be given the chance to audition because the agent will definitely not be calling other agencies to have them submit their clients. It would be a violation of the agent's union franchise to do so. An agent cannot function as a casting director (collecting a fee for casting) and also as a talent agent (collecting a commission from the actors).

Once you have performed in a corporate video, it is a good idea to ask for a videotape copy of your work. Most employers will provide this, perhaps for the cost of a blank tape. Excerpt your scenes, or at least the best ones, and put them on a demo reel that you can then show to other potential employers. When you call the corporations or directors, instead of simply asking if they accept photos, you can ask if they will look at your reel. That implies experience in the field and should help open some doors.

Working in corporate videos is an excellent, low-profile way to develop your camera technique, but a corporate-video demo reel won't be of much use when trying to land an agent unless that agent does a lot of corporate work. He or she will be responsive to a commercial reel, or one with excerpts from films and TV shows, but a corporate-video reel is a very specific kind of thing. It provides currency only when dealing with people in that field.

THE FUTURE OF MULTIMEDIA

The 1996 Telecommunications Reform Act prophesized the ultimate merger of computers, television, and telephone communication, and that is precisely what has been happening. In addition to downloading those games from the Internet, a person can now do grocery shopping from home, take cybertours of the Louvre, purchase airline tickets online, and carry on a dialogue with the children's schoolteachers. Movies with multiple plot lines are here. You can follow particular characters and story developments by directing the action from a clicker while you sit on your sofa. You can send messages back and forth to your friends in Detroit—while looking at their real-time image on your monitor (and while continuing to play a game of computer golf in the upper right-hand corner of your screen!).

Now we have the dawn of "personal television," when viewers can watch what they want, when they want. TiVo, Inc. (www.tivo.com) sells a computerized device that allows the television viewer to pause and fast-forward shows and to totally eliminate commercial interruptions. Want to watch *The Today Show* at midnight instead of when it airs early in the morning? No problem. You simply tell your remote to have it ready for you when you get home. The computer will take care of business for you. Want to accumulate documentaries on the subject of scuba diving? Program it in, and the computer will start collecting them for you. We have traveled several light years from the old *Texaco Hour with Jimmy Durante*. We are rapidly approaching the day when you don't even have to be at home to watch your television shows. We've entered the wireless era, where you can watch what you want when you want on that little device you are carrying in your briefcase, and after you finish watching the show, you can use that same device to call your spouse.

Even the daily newspaper is not the same any more. It used to be that you could get All the News That's Fit to Print in the newspaper that was delivered to your door. No more. Increasingly, you read the paper for the big overview of things and then go online for more in-depth coverage. The *San Jose Mercury News*, just to name one near me geographically, is functioning like this now with its web site, Mercury Center (www.mercurycenter.com). Take a look.

The mind boggles at the possibilities of cyberspace and multimedia. All bets are off. If you can dream it, it will happen. Probably the most significant corporate merger of the past fifty years is the one between computer giant AOL and media conglomerate Time Warner. AOL bought Time Warner, not the other way around. The Internet is buying the movie companies.

Regardless of the shape that the entertainment industry takes in the coming years, we can be sure of this: There is going to be an increasing volume of entertainment production, and with it, an increasing demand for actors. It is up to us to take advantage of the situation.

CHAPTER 9

Auditioning for the Stage

The years I spent in New York doing play after play off-off Broadway and even off-off-off Broadway were at once thrilling and invaluable, and I think of them fondly. The stage is home, and no matter how deeply entrenched you may get in the more lucrative world of film and television, there is always a comfortable feeling going home.

The stage is an *actor's* medium, in contrast to movies, which are generally considered a *director's* medium. This is where all actors are equal, where it is not considered bad form to play a small role in one production and a large one in the next. This is where you can take your best shot at playing Hamlet or Maggie the Cat. It is an arena in which the transaction between actor and audience is at its purest. No one is going to yell "Cut!" if a scene isn't going right, and there is no such thing as a pickup. A theater is a place where we get together to inspire one another, to feed our souls. I have to believe that one day it will be possible to make a decent living in America in this most fragile of art forms.

Michael Shurtleff's *Audition* is the seminal text on the craft of auditioning for stage; if you don't already own a copy, you should. What he has to say about specific techniques actors can use to propel themselves into a cold reading is invaluable, and I have used much of his advice myself. What I want to do here is talk about the differences between an audition for stage and those for the other media. In that regard, there is much to be said.

HOW STAGE PRODUCTIONS ARE CAST

In the theater, the luxury of having a paid casting director isn't always in the budget. You will rarely encounter them in Equity

Waiver (nonpaying) plays or in summer-stock companies, but they are usually present in regional theaters and on Broadway. If a casting director is part of the production, he or she will be intimately familiar with the play being mounted and will function a lot like the casting director for a movie, working closely with the director. The casting director is also going to want to prescreen you if he or she doesn't already know your work.

A prescreen interview for stage offers you the opportunity to present prepared monologues. This is an excellent way for the casting director to get an idea of what you can do, and it gives you the advantage of being able to prepare in advance rather than having to read totally cold from sides. We'll take a close look at monologues and how to select them a little later in this section.

Stage auditions can be held almost anywhere since they don't involve videotape. They might be on a stage or in a drafty rehearsal hall somewhere, but they will invariably be conducted in a location that allows you to move around during your audition, to be physical. This alone makes a stage audition a radically different kind of experience from reading in a cramped production office on a back lot.

Unless you are auditioning to replace a cast member in a long-running show, your audition will invariably be conducted by the actual director. Replacement roles are usually cast by producers and stage managers since the director has moved on to other projects. You will probably be reading with the stage manager instead of the casting director. If a casting director is part of the picture, his or her primary job involves finding the actors and bringing them in. During the readings, the casting director is likely to be sitting next to the director, making notes.

The director is firmly in charge at the auditions. He or she might ask the casting director for information on particular actors and may confer with the producers from time to time, but basically, casting is the director's domain. Everybody wants the director to be happy; once hired, he or she is given wide latitude in casting decisions.

The director's right-hand person is the stage manager, whose job begins with these auditions and extends through the run of the show. Once rehearsals start, the stage manager will keep a record of all blocking and light cues, will make sure props are in place before work begins each day, and will coordinate schedules. When the play opens, the stage manager runs it while the director moves on to other projects. The stage manager has the responsibility of deciding when to hold a curtain, handling emergencies, and making sure the cast is all accounted for at the proper time. You might say the stage manager is a central-control mechanism for the overall production, and he or she represents the director in the latter's absence.

Reading with a stage manager is exactly like reading with a casting director except that, this being stage, he or she will get up and move around with you if the scene requires it. Like a casting director, the stage manager will not "play" the scene, but will give you lines, reading all the parts except yours.

WHAT THE DIRECTOR IS LOOKING FOR

Stage productions enjoy the luxury of rehearsal, and that fact deeply colors what directors look for in the auditions. They know that, once the cast is set, there will be a period of intense experimentation, an opportunity for all the actors to explore their roles in collaboration. Therefore, they don't want to see a final performance at the audition. In fact, if a director thinks he or she is seeing a final performance, a frozen performance, you will likely not be cast.

The image I am most fond of in this context is that of a race horse. The director knows there is going to be a race later on, but right now just wants to see you go around the track a couple of times. He or she wants to learn about your personality as well as your talent; wants to see how physical you are, how agile; what kind of voice you have; how intelligent you are; whether you have a sense of humor; how well you respond to adjustments; what kind of "chemistry" you have with him or her. In addition to casting actors for roles, the director is forming a family that will have to work closely together for a concentrated time, so when auditioning you, he or she is thinking partly about the other members of the cast. This is in dramatic contrast to movies and television, where actors come in, do their thing, and leave, having no real involvement with the rest of the cast or the director. A stage play is an ensemble effort, a piece of art to which everybody contributes. It starts taking shape the first day of rehearsal, but the final form is unknown until it gets in front of an audience. Even then, it continues to evolve.

As with any audition, you should know what your character wants in a scene, where the scene takes place, and what the relationship is between you and the other characters. But on stage, you also want to show your potential. For that, your choices can be dangerously bold. Use humor any place you can. Don't play the obvious choices, play against them. It really does not matter if your audition choices are not appropriate to the character because the director figures you will find the character before opening. What you want to do is show off your moves, your style. You want the director to see as many of your strengths as possible.

HELPFUL HINTS

Following are some concrete suggestions for auditioning for the stage, some things to try and a few to avoid:

- Use the entire stage. If you have a reason to move, do so. Don't stay rooted to the spot. It is visually interesting to see actors turn their backs on the auditors and cross to the upstage wall. Just be sure the move is motivated. I'm not encouraging nervous pacing. Try sitting on the apron of the stage. Sit down and lean against a wall. Remember that words are just part of what is going into the director's brain. What he or she is seeing is vitally important. Try to be visually interesting.
- Hang your hat on relationship and conflict. Remember, conflict is the heart of drama, and comedy too. If in doubt about the relationship between your character and the one you are playing with in a scene, choose love. Actors are warriors of the heart. Act from the heart, not the head.
- Get the words off the script. It drives me crazy to watch an actor following along in his script while the stage manager is reading the other characters. *Listen* to what is being said to you. *React.* Then look in the script for the next line.
- Learn how to deal with physicality in auditions. Kissing scenes and fighting scenes lead actors right down the road to ruin. What you have to learn how to do is "mark" through extreme action. If a scene calls for a tender kiss, try a tender touch on the cheek instead. If it calls for a roundhouse right, try a gentle shove and allow the stage manager to recoil. I have watched actors practically destroy stage managers, scratching and clawing and slugging. The rule is not to get entangled in any way at an audition. You can't deal with the stage manager, your lines, a script, and a fist fight all at the same time.
- Keep the script in your hand and refer to it from time to time,

even if you have received a script in advance and have memorized the scene. A director who sees you playing without a script might think this is as good as you get, that this is a final performance.

- There is strength in keeping a physical distance between the stage manager and yourself. For some reason, actors just love to close in dramatically, to get right up in their scene partner's face. They will invariably do it in a fit of anger, as they rush threateningly toward their partner. Then you can see it flash through their brain that they somehow have to get *out* of the stage manager's face so they can continue the scene. Try looking at it this way: rushing up in your partner's face is equivalent to an exclamation point, so use it sparingly. Anyway, it creates a far stronger visual image and increases tension to play from the opposite side of the stage than your partner.

MONOLOGUES

If you want to act on the stage, sooner or later you'll be asked to bring in those "contrasting monologues," so you might as well get them ready. This is a never-ending task because you'll always be updating them, always keeping an eye out for that special selection that shows you off to just the right advantage. I've seen hundreds of actors present monologues, and I'm fascinated by the generally weak material selected. Too many actors confuse monologues with stand-up routines and cute stories. They come out on stage and muse about something with no particular motivation for the telling. We're not auditioning writers, remember. A good monologue selection is one that causes the actor to *do* something, and if it's physical, all the better.

Let's go back to that image of the actor as a race horse. If you want to show off your best form, you're not just going to stand there in the middle of the field and let them admire you, are you? No, you're going to jump some hurdles, strut a little, maybe hit a gallop. Well, your monologue combination should show you off in the same way.

Usually they ask for contrasting pieces, something classical and something contemporary. Except in Hollywood, where, sadly, some theaters have finally given up asking for classical selections in a movie town and satisfy themselves with contrasting contemporary selections. You should presume, however, that they want classical and contemporary. If you choose a dramatic classical selection, then your contemporary piece should be comedic. If one of them is physical, then the other should be still. Contrast them.

Where can you find these pieces? A good starting point would be my book *The Ultimate Scene and Monologue Sourcebook* (Back Stage Books, 1994), which contains descriptions of over a thousand monologues and scenes, complete with first and last lines, character descriptions, and precise location where the selections can be found within the plays. *The Ultimate Scene and Monologue Sourcebook* is designed specifically for actors who are searching for good scenes and monologues, and it is an excellent reference source.

The entire world of plays and literature is at your disposal when you are looking for monologues. Even though most monologue material comes from stage plays, it's okay to use a passage from a novel if it is written well. Screenplays are dangerous sources, especially if they are from famous movies, because your performance might be compared to whatever Paul Newman or Meryl Streep did. Try to find material that isn't overdone and that shows off your unique qualities. Here are some sample combinations and suggestions about how to proceed.

A good classical selection for an actor would be from *The Tempest,* by Shakespeare, Act II, Scene II. Trinculo, a very pampered court jester, is beside himself with worry over an approaching storm and is trying to find a place to hide. The setup allows the actor to run all over the stage before cozying up next to the smelly savage, Caliban. Very funny stuff, extremely physical.

A nice contrasting contemporary selection would be from *I Never Sang for My Father* by Robert Anderson. At the very end of Act II, Gene turns to the audience and talks about his final visit with his father, trying to express a love he has been unable to put into words. Poignant and still, a perfect accompaniment to *The Tempest.*

As a classical selection, an actress might try the role of Dorine in Molière's *Tartuffe.* In Act II, Scene II, she takes Orgon to task for wanting to marry his daughter Mariane to the scheming Tartuffe. She is saucy, even sassy, full of venom as she makes her case.

Then, as a contrast, try Act I of *The Woolgatherer,* by William Mastrosimone. Rose, having invited an amorous truck driver to her apartment, suddenly surprises him by telling of a terrifying attack on the flamingos at the zoo. Obviously still upset by what she has seen, her descriptions are almost cinematic. Wonderful writing, even if the play is a bit strange, and a good counterpart to Dorine.

By the way, Molière is a fruitful source for actresses in search of monologue material, arguably better than Shakespeare. I have always felt that the men's roles in Shakespeare's plays are stronger than the women's, and I say that knowing I'm going to get angry e-mail. Molière cared about mistreatment of women and made it a recurrent theme. His women are full-blooded, strong, intelligent, and almost always funny. And, of course, we are blessed with Richard Wilbur's wonderful translations. Molière simply seems a fresher choice to me than maybe dusting off Kate from *Taming of the Shrew* once again.

Another Molière play, *The Misanthrope*, has a juicy role in Celimene, and the exchange with her friend Arsinoe in Act III, Scene V, is biting comedy at its best. They cut into each other with claws bared, and Celimene's description of party gossip about Arsinoe is excellent monologue material.

A companion piece might be from *The Fox*, by D. H. Lawrence, adapted for the stage by Allan Miller. Act III, Scene II has Jill trying to warn her companion, Nellie, about the dangers of involvement with Henry. This selection is as heartfelt as Celimene is arch. Nice counterpoint.

Yet another possible combination for an actress would be Lady Anne's speech over Henry's casket in *Richard III*, Act I, Scene II, contrasted with *Division Street* by Steve Tesich, in Act I of which Dinah tells her lawyer, Sal, how attracted she was to Chris, the counterculture sixties leader. The material presents an actress with the opportunity to absolutely chew up the stage if she wants. Terrific stuff.

Prince Hal's scene with his father in Act III, Scene II of *Henry IV, Part I*, is marvelous. Suddenly, the boy becomes a man and promises that the king will be proud of him yet. This is wonderful material for an actor, and it can be contrasted with something like Jonathan's stuttering speech in Act I, Scene II of Arthur Kopit's *Oh Dad, Poor Dad, Mamma's Hung You in the Closet and I'm Feelin' So Sad*, in which he tells Rosalie about his telescope.

Think of your monologue combination as a little three-minute play, complete with a beginning, middle, and end. Consider the overall package when deciding what to do and, just like a good play, build the tension. Pick material that has a clear action to play, something that can involve you immediately, preferably something that allows for physical movement.

It doesn't matter if you combine a contemporary comedy selection with a classical dramatic selection, or a contemporary dramatic selection with a classical comedy selection. The important thing is that your choices contrast with each other. If you have writing talents, feel free to write your own contemporary piece.

You can rewrite, delete, or otherwise alter material to fit your needs, even with Shakespeare. It would be sacrilege to change a word of Arthur Miller or O'Neill in an actual production, but anything goes in an audition. You can construct a monologue out of a scene by eliminating the other character's lines.

If you find something that you like, read the entire play! Do not simply memorize the selection out of the book. Learn something about the character. Be prepared to talk intelligently about your selection if the director wants to. What would you do if, after putting up your piece, the director told you he or she had directed the play your selection was from? If you've read the play and thought about it, you won't be caught off-guard.

PART THREE

THE BUSINESS SIDE OF ACTING

CHAPTER 10

Managing Your Acting Career

If you get in your car and don't have any place to go, you are just going to drive around. The chief executive of every single Fortune 500 company understands this, and that is why their firms operate on five-year plans and long-term projections. Why should the business of acting be any different? Not only is this a business like any other, it is a particularly competitive one, one in which the supply of actors far outstrips the available jobs. Seeking employment as an actor is a bit like selling snow cones in the Antarctic.

Supposedly, over half the people who come into acting as a career get out within three years. I know many talented actors who simply gave up and walked away because they couldn't stomach the business side of the business. On the other hand, I've known more than a few who are arguably lacking in the talent department but who are just good salespeople—and they prosper. Nobody said it was fair.

There is definitely a luck factor to an actor's career. It is always possible to stumble into that one-time role that is the perfect showcase, and it is possible to find yourself sitting next to the head of talent for NBC the next time you are on jury duty. Sure, it's always possible to get hit by a car if you hang around in the street long enough. But that is certainly not a dependable way to get from point A to point B. Wise actors will not depend on luck, but will run their careers as the business it is.

Let's draw an analogy. Suppose you were going into business selling refrigerators. What would you do? Would you just announce to your mom and dad and neighbors that you are in the refrigerator business and then wait for the phone to ring with orders? Of course not. What you would do is make a business plan. You would make sure you have proper office space, a good record-keeping system, an advertising campaign, a sales staff of some kind, and some long-range projections. On the day you open your doors for business, you would have some idea of the number of refrigerators you hope to sell next year.

Now, let's apply the same standard to acting. First of all, you need a good product. Your refrigerator has to work. For the actor, that means you have to develop your craft, to stay in training. It means you have to watch your weight if that's a problem for you, and to resist the urge to start sporting green spiked hair. You want your product to be acceptable to middle America.

You need proper office space. If you were selling refrigerators, you'd probably rent a storefront and display your goods in the window. You'd probably have a desk somewhere in the back of the store. Well, actors don't need a storefront, but they do need a desk area, some place at home that is specifically set aside for business affairs. And they need to make sure that they tend to business in that space every single business day. You need a record-keeping system. Otherwise, how are you going to keep track of what you are doing? Actors meet an incredible number of directors, casting directors, and others—after a few years the names and faces start to blur. A file card setup or database system makes it possible to run a history on each person. I use database divided into categories headed "Agents," "Casting Directors," "TV," "Stage," "Current Projects," and so forth. In each category, I have an entry for each person with whom I want to stay in touch or whom I want to remember. I even include information like whether a person is fat or skinny, a smoker or not, loud or not, cerebral or not, funny or not. That way, when you get an audition, you can check your references for an update on the people you'll be seeing.

Your record-keeping system should also have some way of tracking your own residual payments from commercials and such. Get a ledger book and ask someone at the union to show you how to log in payments when you start getting them. That way, at year end you'll be able to compare your figures against the W-2s you'll get. This system will also help you keep track of which W-2s are still outstanding. It isn't uncommon for actors to have as many as twenty different employers in the course of a year.

You need an advertising campaign. For the actor, this means having good photos, picture postcards, promotional flyers, maybe a web site. From time to time, you may want to place notice of a play or movie credit in trade publications.

In addition, you would probably employ some commissioned salesmen to sell your refrigerators. Actors' commissioned salesmen are called talent agents, and you should make it your business to work with good ones. Even when you have them, however, never forget that this is *your* career we are talking about, and you should never give control of your career over to anyone else. If you were selling those refrigerators, you wouldn't let the salesmen out front run your business, would you? It is your responsibility to keep up with industry trends, to read trade publications, local and national, such as *Hollywood Reporter, Backstage West-DramaLogue, Daily Variety, American Theatre Magazine,* maybe even the Sunday *New York Times.* You have to find out what is happening in the marketplace and then initiate activity. Don't just sit there waiting for the phone calls from your agents.

You need long-range projections. What do you want to be doing five years from now? Movies? Television? Commercials? A combination? How much money do you want to be making? If you want to make it happen, you should have a plan. What you need to do is work backward, starting five years from now. The reasoning goes this way: in order to be where I want to be five years from now, where do I have to be four years from now? In order to be where I want to be four years from now, where do I have to be three years from now? Two years? One year? Six months from now? One month from now? If I want to be where I should be one week from now, what should I be doing today to get me there?

By applying business standards to the acting profession, you will avoid the extreme emotional highs and lows. If you sold a refrigerator, that would be good news, but it wouldn't be occasion to close up shop and vacation in the Bahamas for a month. It would be another wonderful sale, and would hopefully lead to others. By the same token, if your refrigerators were not selling, if you hit a dry spell (and, take it from me, you will), you would know that an adjustment to your game plan was necessary. Maybe you would devise a new promotional drive, do a special mailing, get new pictures made. The thing you wouldn't do is go spinning into abject depression because of the lack of sales. Your commitment to your profession would be based on firmer ground.

Several years ago, the National Sales Executive Association released some figures that I think have specific relevance for actors. The figures were based on just such activities as selling refrigerators.

- 80 percent of all sales in the country are made after the fifth call on the same prospect.
- 48 percent of all salesmen make one call and cross the prospect off.
- 25 percent quit after the second call.
- 12 percent call three times and quit.
- 10 percent keep calling. On a national average, 10 percent of all salesmen make 80 percent of the sales.

To me, these figures speak of the value of long-term commitment and organized persistence, and I can think of nothing more important for the actor to consider. Try thinking of it this way: the business of acting is the search for employment. The acting is the fun part. Keep your eye on the target, and you have a decent chance of hitting it.

CHAPTER 11

Finding and Keeping an Agent

Agents are actors' brokers, their representative in the marketplace. If you want to make money from acting, you have to have at least one, maybe two or three, and the quest for this representation can be a source of career-long anxiety. An agent is technically employed by an actor to provide a service; that's why the IRS says that agents' commissions are deductible on your taxes. That fact would suggest that you could therefore simply go out and hire one, but in the real world it's not as easy as that. The Catch-22 is that the easiest agents to secure are frequently the lowest ones on the totem pole. The really excellent agencies, the ones whose clients are seen for all the best work, seem always to have a full client list, not needing new people, and anyway they are too busy to set up general interviews. I can think of very few actors who have not at one time or another felt like banging their head against a wall over this issue. Good news: you can get good representation if you want to and are willing to persist with the effort. The trick is to be organized and smart about the pursuit, to look at the big picture.

HOW AGENTS WORK

Outside New York and Los Angeles, franchised agencies are universally "full service." That means they represent performers for theatrical work as well as commercials, and they may handle children as well as adults. They may even have a fashion modeling and print department. In Hollywood, most agencies specialize either in theatrical (film/TV/stage) or commercial representation, and a performer who wants to work in both arenas has to have two different agents. In New York, there are both specialty and full-service agencies. How do you know if an agency is full service or not? Check its franchises. You can call your local SAG office or go to the union's web site (www.sag.org) for a list indicating an agency's specialties, if any.

If you are pursuing acting work in any sizable city, it is very important that you restrict your search for an agent only to those franchised by the performers' unions. They have signed agreements with SAG, AFTRA, and AEA that allow them to represent union performers in exchange for abiding by fairly extensive rules and regulations set down by the unions to protect performers. They also agree not to take more than 10 percent commission on an actor's earnings. Any person who is seriously interested in acting as a career would be a fool to sign up with a nonfranchised agent for the simple reason that the unions have a hammerlock on the business.

In Los Angeles there are more than 200 franchised agents, and in New York a bit over half that. There are franchised agents in virtually every major city, including San Francisco, Detroit, Dallas, and Atlanta, so unless you live in a remote area, you should have access to one or more.

Before you start pursuing them, you should consider the distinctions between commercial and theatrical agents because this will color your approach. A commercial agent is mightily influenced by physical type and a winning personality. If you don't have an extensive acting background, it's not the end of the world from their perspective. As we've already seen, many nonactors do get cast in commercials. Therefore, it's not unusual for a commercial agent smitten with a nonactor to offer representation and merely suggest that the person take a commercial auditioning workshop. Theatrical agents, on the other hand, have to know that you can actually act. Yes, they are influenced by type, but they can't be sending nonactors to stage or movie auditions, so they are not going to represent you unless they are satisfied that you can deliver the goods.

A theatrical agency will represent far fewer actors than will a commercial agency, probably fifty on average as opposed to an average of five hundred in the major markets, so this kind of representation is more difficult to obtain. Many performers who have done a lot of commercials still can't seem to get a good theatrical agent.

Full-service agencies vary dramatically in size, ranging from a company with only one or two agents to huge operations with several agents handling commercials and several more handling theatrical all under the same roof. If you live outside New York and Los Angeles, the odds are that full-service agencies you pursue will employ fewer agents and will earn most of their commissions from commercials, not theatrical. This is important to remember because, though they will have an eye on your acting credentials, they have their bankbook geared to commercials. The fastest way to representation in those companies is to fit into their commercial criteria. More on that later.

SETTING UP AN INTERVIEW

No matter where you live, there is a standard procedure suggested for approaching agents. It is entirely possible, even likely, that this effort will not get you over the wall of the fortress the first time, and you may have to regroup and try again. Primarily, this is due to the huge volume of aspiring actors trying to gain entrance, and you shouldn't let it bother you.

First, make sure you have a good 8x10 photo. (See "Theatrical Photos and Resumes," pages 128–34.) Obtain the current list of franchised agents from the Screen Actors Guild. Be very cautious about "talent agencies" or "model agencies" that run display ads in the Yellow Pages. Often these places are schools masquerading as legit agencies. You're better off sticking with the list from the unions. If you live in L.A. or New York, you might also want to visit a theatrical book store and purchase one of the publications that include names of specific agents within the agencies and editorial comment about agency specialties. This way you can cut down the list to a nice neat thirty or so that could be considered prime candidates. Send your photo and resume (if you have one) to as many agents as you want simultaneously. You don't have to wait for a response from one before approaching another. Be sure to send the material to specific people, not simply to agencies, and it is okay to address agents by their first names.

In cities outside New York and Hollywood, some talent agencies make a practice of responding to submissions with a form letter if a self-addressed, stamped envelope is enclosed. For my money, this is a big fat waste of time. If an agent likes the materials you sent in the mail, believes you have a good look and, based on your photo, thinks he or she can generate some work for you, then the agent is going to call you in for an interview, right? If the agent doesn't like the materials, then what difference does a form letter rejection make anyway? I prefer the way things work in the two major cities, even if it seems cold. There, you send in your materials and just presume they are likely to wind up in the trash can—and you proceed anyway.

At any rate, even if you receive a form letter rejection in the mail, you cannot presume you have in fact been rejected. All it means is that you didn't get an interview yet. You have no way of knowing who saw your photo or whether anybody actually looked at it at all. The more likely scenario is that your submission will either result in a prompt telephone call from the agency secretary, wanting to set up an interview for you—or with silence, no response at all. If no one from the agency has called you within a week or so, you should call the agency. When the receptionist answers, ask to speak to the person you sent the photo to. If the receptionist asks what you want, say that it is regarding representation and that you've already sent a photo and resume. The response will almost certainly be: "We don't represent people who aren't in the union," or "We already have too many actors of your type," or "We look at photos every third Friday; if there is interest, we'll be in touch," or "We are too busy at the present time to hold interviews. Try again in a few months." It all adds up to the infamous "Don't call us, we'll call you."

All right, now what? You've done all the right things, gone by the book, and have come up empty-handed. Here's where the wheat starts separating from the chaff, acting-wise. It's time to regroup. You'll have to try an alternative approach.

THE SECOND APPROACH

All you can really be certain of at this point is that you don't have an interview. Silence and/or form letters do not mean your career is over. Your photo might still be sitting on a desk with two hundred others, still in unopened envelopes. These people can receive as many as twenty-five pictures a day, and it is entirely possible they simply have not gotten to you yet. Or it may have been tossed in the trash. I have watched my own agents sort through the daily incoming photos, and it is a sobering experience. They will open an envelope, pull out the picture, glance at it for maybe four seconds and make a snap decision, either putting it in a "to be called" stack or in the trash. It is a knee-jerk response to the overwhelming volume of aspiring actors.

If three weeks go by and you still haven't heard anything, you can safely conclude that you made it to the trash can and start trying to figure out why. If your approach was to a theatrical agent, you were probably passed on because you either lacked sufficient acting background or are physically too much like other actors the agent represents. Remember, he or she is only going to represent a relatively few actors and doesn't want too much duplication on the client list. A commercial agent likely passed on you because you did not fit into a definable type category, or you fall into the most populated one. I asked one of Hollywood's busiest commercial casting directors to break down the basic type categories of actors, knowing this would be her criteria when talking to agents. Here is her list:

- Kids, 4 to 6, 7 to 10, and 10 to 12 years old
- Teenagers, 13 to 17
- College types, 18 to 22; preppy, bright
- Young professionals, 25 to 40; white-collar males and females who live in a metropolitan area
- Nice Midwest moms and dads, 28 to 32
- Jocks, 26 to 36; outdoorsy guys, beer drinkers
- Spokesmen and women, 35 to 55; good looking, solid, able to handle a lot of dialogue
- Beautiful people, 18 to 25; models fall into this category
- Blue-collar character men, 28 to 55
- Character, comedic men and women 35 to 55
- Handsome, late-middle-aged men and women, including doctors, lawyers, chairs of the board, executives
- Ethnic types, Asian and Hispanic, all ages
- Grandma and Grandpa

Notice that there isn't a category for regular-looking people in the eighteen- to forty-nine-year-old age group, which is the main target audience for TV. Isn't that interesting? It surely can't be that there aren't any people in that group, because it is the most populous of all. What it means is that, even if you fall in this group, you still must fit into a type category as defined by the casting directors and agents.

"But, I don't want to be typed," you may protest. "I'm an actor and can play all kinds of different roles!" Before you get too worked up over this, put yourself back in the agent's seat for a minute as he or she is going through that stack of photos, looking at prospective new clients, and balancing what he or she sees against a mental checklist of types exactly like the one above. If an agent can't categorize you immediately, he or she will surely pass on you.

Maybe the picture you sent in is too middle-of-the-road. What would happen if you wore glasses? If you wore a business suit instead of a sweater-shirt combo? How about if you got a haircut? Went from blonde to brunette? Got rid of the toupee? Shaved your mustache? Is your existing picture sending a mixed message? If you are a woman over thirty and you are still wearing hair down to your waist, that is a mixed message. Hair that long is for young girls. Anyway, it is better to be on the younger end of an older type category. That way you will age gracefully into it. If you are thirty trying to pass yourself off as early twenties, it will only become an increasingly difficult trick. Also, you will be competing at auditions with women who are truly in their early twenties. In general, if you are going to fudge on your age, it is smarter to fudge older, not younger—even if you are convinced that there is more work for the younger actors.

For a second approach, you might want to try edging yourself into a new type category and have new photos taken. Maybe you want a down-the-middle headshot in addition to a couple of shots that firmly categorize you type-wise. It's perfectly all right to send more than one picture in the packet. (I would advise against a composite at this point, however. See "Theatrical Photos and Resumes," pages 131–32.)

Go ahead and send your new pictures to the same group of agents you hit the first time, and see what happens. Don't worry that they might remember your first submission. They won't. Between then and now, they've seen another eight thousand pictures and you didn't make that much of an impression the first time around anyway.

If there is no response within a week, start calling just as before. Only this time, try calling at different times of the day than you did last time. Receptionists work a fairly structured schedule, so try calling early in the morning or after five. You might luck out and get one of the agents on the phone. Remember, keep notes on your 3x5 cards of each effort to make contact.

IF YOU STILL CAN'T GET THROUGH

Still can't get through? Okay, try this: send a personal, short, handwritten note to the agent you originally wrote to. Enclose a resume but, instead of an 8x10 photo, use a picture postcard. (See "Theatrical Photos and Resumes," pages 133–34). Send it all in a letter-sized envelope. That way, when the morning mail arrives, your letter will go into a different stack than the usual twenty 8x10 envelopes. You can be pretty certain that the actual agent will read this one. Your note should say something like, "Dear Linda: I sent in my photo and resume a while back, but I got stopped by your agency moat. Congratulations on having the most efficient staff in town. Still, I want to meet you. You are a top agent, and I think we might work well together. How about a chat?"

If the agent doesn't respond to that, you are dealing with a person who is hard-core. Try sending a telegram. Be cute and brief. If that doesn't work, start all over again, this time pursuing another agent within the agency who might have a more receptive personality. And you can always try simply dropping by the agency, but you will probably meet the same receptionist you've been talking to on the phone. Anyway, dropping by is more of a New York phenomena because "making rounds" is a way of life there; people don't do that in Hollywood very much.

No matter how hard an agent may be to reach, it can be done. I have never seen anybody not get through if he or she really wanted to and was persistent. The acting business is not like a department store—there isn't a personnel director who automatically interviews anybody who sends in an application. Actors are essentially applying for jobs where no openings exist. You can't let that stop you. It is simply not an option not to obtain good representation, so you'll just have to keep trying until you prevail.

Here's a hot tip: Keep an eye peeled for the opening of new talent agencies. When an agency opens its doors for business, the owners usually announce the fact to the trade via ads in industry publications like *Backstage* and *Variety*. This is absolutely the best time to go after them. You know for certain that they don't have a client list yet and have to build one, so they'll be more receptive to new people. Just be sure that the new agencies you pursue are staffed by experienced agents rather than people who are making an initial foray into show biz. You don't want to sign up with someone who has been selling Toyotas and has decided to give actors a whirl. You need someone who has established contacts with the casting directors.

THE INTERVIEW

Congratulations! You got the interview. Now what? It was hard to get, and you don't want to waste it. Here's what you can expect to happen when you get to the agency: if your interview is with a full-service or commercial agency, the agent will chat with you briefly, look at your resume or discuss your lack of one, and may give you some commercial copy to read—and might put your audition on videotape for others in the agency to see. Hopefully, the agent will introduce you to his or her associates. Finally, you'll be told that the agent and those associates will pow-wow and will let you know one way or the other in a day or two. In rare instances, you'll get a thumbs up or down right there on the spot.

An interview with a theatrical agent will also consist of a chat, and if he or she doesn't know your work, maybe the opportunity to do your monologues in the office. Introductions all around, and they will let you know in a day or two.

Before setting out for the interview, be sure you are dressed to fit your type category and that you look like your picture. Also, remember that an interview of this sort has the same dynamic as a commercial audition. High energy, positive sense of life.

If the agent asks you to read copy, read directly to the agent as if he or she were the camera; play as if the agent were scene partner. A few agents might tell you not to do this because it makes them uncomfortable. Okay, then talk to something inanimate near their heads.

Remember that everybody wants a winner. You want to give the impression that you will work with or without this agent, but you don't want to be cocky or arrogant about it. If you must, play mental tricks on yourself. Pretend you already have four commercials on the air, and assume that dynamic. The important thing is that you absolutely do not want to be dealing with the agent in a deferential way. He or she is your equal!

Try to anticipate the trickiest questions so you can have positive answers for them. For example, "What have you done?" is a stopper for a lot of beginning actors. If you are inexperienced, it is easy to get defensive about it. (My favorite answer was given by a New York friend. When a casting director asked him that, he said, "Why? Do you smell something?" I wouldn't go that far.) A good answer might be that you've been taking classes and auditioning for plays and student films, that you've been really busy. Don't just sit there and look like a waif. Don't let them think that your main activity for the past six months has been trying to meet agents.

If you are a nonactor, one of the most important things you can communicate to the agent is how serious you are about acting. Don't bring the subject up, but if you're asked about your day job, say that there is zero problem getting off to go to auditions, that your major interest in life is acting, and that you have structured your schedule to allow for that priority. Do not waffle on this point! I saw one new actress cost herself an agent because she insisted on discussing her day job with him. The agent doesn't care if you are a brain surgeon and the president is one of your patients. He or she only wants to know if you can be counted on to arrive on time for the toothpaste commercial.

If your interview is with a theatrical agency, there will be a different dynamic. You and the agent will chat, but you don't have to treat the meeting like a commercial audition. It is okay to kick back a bit. Hopefully, the agent will already know your work from seeing you in a play or a student film. If not, you may get the opportunity to do your monologues in the office. The agent is not apt to spring this on you by surprise, though. When your appointment is first set, the receptionist will tell you if they expect you to perform in the office. Since a monologue can tell only part of the story, an agent will sometimes ask you to put up a scene instead and will schedule a second appointment time for that. If you run into that situation, keep these points in mind: (1) This is your audition, not your scene partner's. If you can, find a scene that is equally balanced, but at the very least you should play the showier role. (2) All the rules that apply to selecting stage monologue material apply here. Avoid plays that are too familiar or that have been made into a well-known movie. (3) The scene should be contemporary instead of classical, and should not be more than three or four minute long. (4) If you have reason to believe that the agency in question does more television work than movie work, choose a comedic scene. If the agency is stage-oriented or does a lot of movies, you can get away with drama. After all the meetings and/or office auditions are over, the agent will let you know in a day or two whether the agency wants to represent you.

EXCLUSIVITY VERSUS FREELANCE REPRESENTATION

During the years I lived and worked in New York, I freelanced. That is, I did not sign a contract with a single agent, preferring to accept auditions and jobs through any who would call me. I "made rounds" of the agencies, staying in touch with several on an almost daily basis. After moving to Hollywood, I signed exclusive contracts with specialty agencies, one for commercials and one for theatrical, because that is what the unions require in that city. Today I even have a third agent, one for voice work. In my opinion, it really doesn't matter if you are signed for exclusive representation just as long as you are getting auditions and work. You do whatever the marketplace demands, and there are arguments pro and con regarding exclusivity.

Pro: If you are exclusive with an agent, he or she will take more of an interest in your career than if you are a freelance client. Because you are signed exclusively, the agent will try harder to find you work.

Con: By signing exclusively with an agent, you are giving away a bit of your autonomy. You can't play agents off against one another, making each of them believe that the others think you are hot stuff. If you are signed exclusively, you may have to compete within your own agency for spots at the audition, especially if the agent has several actors in your type category under contract.

Personally, I like the freedom of freelancing, but I wouldn't stand in fire to defend it. For one thing, theatrical work is much harder to find if you are freelancing than if you are signed. For another, even if you sign exclusive contracts, they are really written to protect the actor. If you don't make money, you can break it anyway. If you are making money, why would you want to break it?

A problem might arise if you live in a city where all the agencies are small full-service companies, and one of them wants to sign you. If the agent is very strong commercially but weak theatrically, it could be a bad move to sign across the board. On the other hand, the agent might not take you at all unless you sign across the board. If confronted with such a situation, and if I was certain that I was dealing with one of the better agents in town, I would probably sign even if I was opposed to it in principle. I'd give it a year and see what happens. If I work, terrific; if not, I can always move on.

CHANGING AGENTS

There are a lot of reasons for changing agents. Maybe your hottest agent at the agency has left for another agency. Maybe you haven't had an audition in six months. Maybe you just don't have good chemistry with your agent. There is no easy way to do it, but everybody understands that it is done. Nothing personal. Be friendly, and don't burn any bridges. The day may come when you and the agent will work together again. I strongly advise you not to leave in a huff.

Also, don't leave one agent before finding another. It is accepted practice to be interviewing with other agents if you are not getting work, and you don't need to be defensive about it. It is unlikely that the agents you are seeing will call your current agent and tell on you.

Sometimes it is necessary to change agents in order to get better roles. In Hollywood, some agents specialize in the smaller "day player" roles, and some work on leads and contract parts. If you have worked like a bandit at the day roles, one of the other agents might get interested in you. You'd wind up with fewer auditions, but for better stuff. Mind you, changing agents for this reason is guaranteed to irritate the agent you are leaving if he or she knows why you are going, so my advice is not to spell it out.

SOME PARTING THOUGHTS ON FINDING AND KEEPING AN AGENT

When you are pursuing agents, be nice to the receptionists. They are doing the best they can. Theirs must be one of the most awful jobs in the entire world. Nobody in their right mind could *like* fighting off actors.

The fastest way to meet any agent is via personal introduction. If you know somebody in the biz who can help you, don't hesitate to ask. Sometimes, it really is "who you know."

Never use trickery to gain an interview. I know one guy, a lawyer trying to break into acting, who sent agents subpoenas. Bad move. Another fellow identified himself to the receptionist as a former college buddy of the agent. He got through all right, but he just made the agent mad. Also, avoid trying anything risqué or in bad taste. By all means, be inventive, but keep in mind that you are going to have to live with whatever you do. Vulgarity is a bad idea. Don't be like the actor who sent a female agent one silk stocking and a note explaining she could have the other one in exchange for an interview.

CHAPTER 12

Theatrical Photos and Resumes

"**F**ish got to swim, birds got to fly . . ." and actors got to have photos. I suppose that is why I have seen more money wasted in this area than in any other. Your theatrical photo and resume are primary tools of your trade. Because you'll be sending them to agents and casting directors, it is crucial that both be prepared just right. The first thing to understand is that a theatrical photo is not like the picture of you sitting on the mantel at home. Stay away from neighborhood portrait studios and hide from Uncle Howie and his Minolta. You want to make certain that you get your pictures taken only by knowledgeable theater professionals.

The mistakes you can make with your photo fall into three categories: (1) bad photographer; (2) good photos that don't look like you; (3) bad reproduction. The best way to find a good photographer is to ask other actors who takes their pictures. Also, you can conduct your own little telephone poll of franchised agents in your city, asking each of them who they recommend to their clients. You'll start hearing the same names pop up again and again. Make some appointments with the photographers so you can drop by for a chat. Look at their work. You should have a gut feeling about whether you are in the right place or not. Trust it. If the photographer seems to be intimidating to you, or if you think he or she is charging too much, move along. If you aren't comfortable with the person, you will not get a good session.

A HEADSHOT THAT SELLS

At minimum, you need one excellent gangbusters headshot, a picture that looks exactly like you. It should show not only where you fit in terms of type, but also what is special and different about you. Agents see a lot of pictures. You need to stand out from the crowd.

An actress once gave me a picture for feedback and, to tell the truth, if she hadn't been standing right there in front of me, I wouldn't have known she was the person in the shot. In life, she wore glasses and was roughly fifteen pounds overweight. Her complexion was freckly and her hair was flaming red. The photo, on the other hand, was shot so that her hair appeared brunette, she wasn't wearing the glasses, but was wearing too much eye makeup, and she evidently had the session before she gained the weight. Also, the girl in the picture was coming on like some kind of French movie, and the strongest quality of the real-life subject was an energetic, childlike innocence.

Not only was this actress walking around with a picture that was no good, she was actually in danger of making influential people angry. Someone who looked at that shot and called the actress in for an interview would not be happy when someone else walked in. She would have been in trouble even before shaking hands.

Maybe the problem comes from the mistaken perception that professional theatrical pictures should be glamorous, should somehow fit a glamorous industry. Maybe every aspiring actress sees herself as a budding Marilyn Monroe, and every actor as Marlon Brando. I only know that I see a lot of pictures that don't look like the people who posed for them, and there is no question that such pictures are a bad mistake.

TYPING YOURSELF

Go back and review that list of type categories in the previous chapter on agents (page 121). Do you know where you fit? If not, try this: Watch some TV shows that are aimed at your demographic age group. If you are in your late twenties to early forties, for instance, watch the early morning talk shows, or maybe *ER*, programs that are aimed at working professionals and their families. But here's the trick: Don't pay any attention to the show itself. Instead, watch the commercials. That's where your competition lives. You'll see plenty of spots featuring white-collar working people, many of whom are juggling family and job. Get the idea? If you are in your late teens or early twenties, watch prime-time shows like *Friends*. If you are in your sixties, watch *60*

Minutes. But remember: Watch the commercials, not the show. Note how the actors in the commercials are dressed, how their hair is cut, what their basic dynamic is. This will help you get an idea of what your own commercial type might be.

A good headshot is one that is shot on black-and-white film, preferably Plus-X or slower, with ample lighting. There shouldn't be a lot of shadows or back lighting. Most important, the essential personality trait of the subject should be evident in the photo. In other words, we want to be looking at a picture of who the actor is right now, not who he or she would like to be, or can make himself or herself up to be in a crunch. Don't be too artsy with these things. And the actor should be *relating* to the camera, not posing for it. When you relate to the lens of the camera as if it is a person who might talk back to you, it will cause your eyes to "jump out" of the shot.

It doesn't make much difference whether the picture is taken outdoors or in a studio. Many photographers prefer to work in studio because it gives them more control over the lighting, and that is a perfectly good reason. The picture I am using now was shot inside, but one I used to use was shot outside.

As for what to wear, take your cue from commercials if the shot will be used for that purpose or if you are trying to land a full-service agent. Stay with muted colors, no turtlenecks, spare jewelry. A jacket and tie is okay for men, but it is limiting. I favor a simple, open-neck sport shirt. The idea is to convey a sense of happy energy, confidence. If your picture is going to be used for purely theatrical purposes, the dress doesn't matter as much as the attitude. You don't need to stress animation so much in a theatrical shot. When a casting director looks at it, a good theatrical photo should convey the message: "I know what I'm doing, and I like who I am; you know what you are doing. Let's get together and work on a project." I would only advise against wearing anything that is too sexy, low cut, or otherwise revealing.

Whether the photo is for commercial or for theatrical purposes, be warned against making your hair the star of the picture if you happen to own a gorgeous mane. They are not casting hair.

Makeup artists are an optional matter. Some photographers include the services of one in their basic fee, and that's okay. I've personally never needed one, but then most men are going to wear only a pancake base and no eye makeup at all. Women might feel better if there is someone there to keep an eye on their hair and to make sure their forehead isn't shining. The only problem I see with this is the possibility that a makeup artist can make the actor look *too* perfect. It's not wonderful to have absolutely every hair in place. It doesn't look natural. (That's what is wrong with the picture your mom has on the mantel.)

Be very careful when touching up your photo. It is one thing to airbrush out a pimple that would go away in a day or two by itself, and it's quite another to cause a scar to disappear. Again, you need to look *exactly* like your photo. No wishful thinking. Don't be airbrushing out your wonderful age wrinkles. They look good and are a sign of experience. Leave them alone.

COMPOSITES

Composites are used only for commercials. You would not want to include a photo of yourself playing Lady Macbeth on a composite. The typical composite has a headshot on one side of the paper and on the other, three to five other situational shots. The idea is that it allows you to show an ad agency a lot of different roles you might be able to play.

I don't believe that you need a composite in order to get work. I didn't use one in New York and it never hurt me. On the other hand, I have used one off and on in Hollywood, at the suggestion of various agents, and I haven't seen a significant increase in jobs. Mainly, composites are expensive. However, if the agents in your city insist on them, go ahead and get one made. I'm not using one at the present time. Instead, I have two different 8x10 headshots, one very lighthearted and the other more severe. If I'm up for a hard-nosed attorney in a movie, I give them the stern shot; if I'm up for a commercial, I use the nice one.

If you do use a composite, each situational shot should show a different way you can be cast in commercials. You might want a picture of you as a schoolteacher, another of you as a flight attendant, and another of you digging in the rose garden at home. They should be situational rather than presentational. The school teacher should be drying a child's tear, the flight attendant should be fluffing a pillow, that kind of thing. For some reason many photographers do not give good guidance in this area. I've seen many composites where the actor is merely posed wearing different clothes in each shot, but not involved in any activity, and they look very stilted. Remember, too, that the picture should feature you, not a product. You don't want to be photographed standing there grinning over a can of Coke. It would be better to be pouring the Coke for a friend. Get it?

Be inventive when choosing composite shots. A telephone-repair*woman* climbing up a telephone pole is a wonderful shot because it surprises. A man taking a casserole out of the oven works for the same reason. I saw a clever composite shot in which a fellow had trapped a butterfly on his head with a net. Try to show some style with your pictures. I've seen actors also use the composite format for very original promotional purposes. One fellow has his headshot on the front and a picture of the back of his head on the back. Another has his baby pictures on the back. These things are fun, but I would use them as an addendum, not as your mainstay composite.

In New York and Hollywood, color shots will label you as a beginner, so don't use them. They are expensive to shoot and reproduce, and they won't get you any more work. You might be able to upload one into your web site, but that's a different matter. We're talking about regular headshots here, the ones you hand out at auditions. Models sometimes use color shots in their portfolios, but actors don't need them. In some of the smaller cities there are a few agents who like color shots, but if you head for the major leagues, switch to black-and-white fast.

WHAT TO SPEND ON PHOTOS

How much to spend varies a lot with where you live, but generally you can expect to pay a photographer between $200 and $300 for a session involving one or two roles of film and yields a single headshot. A composite session can cost anywhere from $450 all the way up to $700 or so. It depends on how many locations are involved, how many rolls of film, how much time.

After your photo session, the photographer will have the film developed and printed on contact sheets—one roll of film per sheet. The individual shots are printed too small to see clearly with the naked eye, so you need to use a magnifying glass. A popular instrument made especially for this purpose is the Agfa Lupe 8x, which is available inexpensively at any photo supply store. Once you have selected the shots you would like to see enlarged, the photographer usually has that done for you. By the time you get them back, they have been airbrushed, if such improvements are needed. On rare occasions the photographer will simply give you the roll of film after a session and let you take care of getting your own enlargements at a lab. Whatever the procedure, you'll eventually wind up with 8x10 photos in your hand. At that point, you'll have to make some decisions about whether to have them reproduced with standard photo duplication or lithography. Composites, which are typically run off in bulk numbers, are almost always reproduced with a lithographic process on a special paper because this is the cheaper way to go. You can get five hundred lithographic copies of a photo for what one hundred will cost you using photo duplication. Plan on spending at least $250 for five hundred copies of your composite on lithography. Standard photo lab duplication, which is how many actors like to reproduce their theatrical headshots, cost substantially more. You can expect to spend $1 per copy, or more. Plus, you'll have another $125 of setup costs for the first run. The lab takes a picture of the 8x10 photo that you bring in, making a new 8x10 negative. Then they use this negative to run off the number of photos you are ordering.

There are no firm rules about whether photo duplication or lithography is the better process. I like photo lab duplication for my headshots because the resulting reproductions seem more upscale to me, and because I think they hold skin tone better than lithography, which tends to make black and white contrasts a bit too stark for my taste. But I have seen a lot of perfectly fine lithography.

Note: When you finally have a stack of one hundred, or five hundred, photos sitting in front of you, you will see that the copies are not quite as clear and sharp as the original you had them struck from. Your duplicates are never going to look as good as your original because they are pictures of pictures. You are down a generation from the original shot you gave to the photo lab. This is a good reason to ask to see a proof before the lab proceeds to run off hundreds of them. The lab will make the 8x10 negative and run off a single shot with several different contrast levels. You can pick the one you think is the most flattering. If you do not elect to see a proof, it is presumed you are going to trust the lab technicians to use their own judgment.

POSTCARDS

Postcards are worth their weight in platinum. You can get them at the same place you order composites. Postcards are almost always reproduced with lithography, though photo labs will do them too. You will have your choice of a bewildering array of sizes and styles, and you will have to choose a font style for your name slug, which goes on the postcard. I personally like my post-cards to measure 4x6 since they will fit into a #10 letter-sized envelope. That way I can use them for reaching hard-to-get-to people, like agents and directors. I have discovered that casting offices make nice neat stacks of 8x10 envelopes, which come in by the bushel-basketful, but they will usually open letter-sized envelopes right away.

Once you have the postcards in your hot little hands, you should develop the practice of sending one to everybody you want to stay in touch with—every three or four weeks. It doesn't matter what you write on them. These are not "the weather's nice, wish you were here" postcards. Just write "Hiya" if you want. The point is to hit people like casting directors with your face again and again until they finally remember who you are. These are a simply wonderful investment, and I can directly trace many auditions and jobs to their use.

You can also make excellent use of specialty postcards. For example, shortly before my permanent move from New York to Los Angeles, I shot a commercial for a bank, and the motif was post–Civil War. I was a carpetbagger and was given a terrific cos-tume. We shot the spot on a farm out on Long Island somewhere. During a break on the set, I gave the camera I had brought with me to one of the camera operators, who ran off a few shots of me posing on a buckboard that was gathering dust nearby. I happily doffed my carpetbagger top hat high above my head in greeting. The next day I went to a photo lab to have the roll of film devel-oped, and when that was accomplished I had the words "ED HOOKS HEADING WEST!!" inserted on the front of that buckboard. The result was a humorous, fully costumed photo that I turned into a postcard, sending it to all the casting directors and agents I could think of in L.A. It worked. When I got off the plane at LAX and checked my service, I had calls waiting for me from several agents, one of whom I wound up signing with.

THEATRICAL RESUMES

The theatrical resume is an actor's calling card, a form of intro-duction, something we run off by the hundreds and attach to our photos. It is not the kind of formal submission you might make to the personnel department of a Fortune 500 company.

You'll get different advice from different folks about how these things should look—whether to list the precise roles you have played, whether to write down an age range, whether to mention that you wear contact lenses, and so on. I'm offering the resume of my friend Smith Dane as a good guideline. Smith has credits on both coasts, has studied with some good people, and is a union member. Even if you don't have his extensive credits, the format remains the same.

Only theatrically relevant information should be on a theatrical resume. The fact that you hold a law degree or a Ph.D. in astrophysics is impressive but is not theatrically important. It means much more to a casting director or an agent that you studied for six months with Stella Adler or Sanford Meisner than it does that you once received the Silver Cross for bravery. They want to know what actual experience you have had performing and with whom you have studied, and that's about it. (One proviso: If you have advanced training in something that might be profitable theatrically, mention it. For instance, when a licensed psychiatrist was enrolled in one of my acting classes, I advised him to mention that because he might at some point manage to get an on-camera gig as a mental-health expert.)

Resumes for New York actors generally look very much like those for Hollywood actors, except that on the East Coast they like to put stage credits on top; in Los Angeles, agents and casting directors want to see movies and TV credits first. You should follow the practice and custom of whatever format is popular in your own city. If you are bicoastal then maintain two resumes, one for each coast.

If you have zero acting credits, then I suggest you do not prepare a resume at all. Instead, when you send your photo out to agents and casting directors, attach a letter summarizing your experience. "I'm currently studying with Ed Hooks and am seeking representation." or "After retiring from a successful career in nursing, I am happily reaching for the brass ring of acting. I've been studying acting technique with Ed Hooks for six months and have taken several commercial workshops. Ed says you are a terrific agent, and I'd love to meet you," that kind of thing. Then get busy with developing a resume. Try to get cast in short-run plays, student films, staged readings, whatever you can do that is theatrical and brief. You'll be surprised at how rapidly you can fill a page with resume credits if you try.

SMITH DANE

Contact: Terry Lichtman Co.
(818) 783-3003
SAG/AFTRA/AEA

Ht: 5'11"
Wt: 165
Hair: Brown

FILMS

RAISING CAIN	Brian De Palma
METRO	Thomas Carter
HEART AND SOULS	Ron Underwood
STRIKING DISTANCE	Rowdy Herrington
DEFENSELESS	Martin Campbell
HANNIBAL	Ridley Scott

TELEVISION

FRIENDS	Seymour Robbie
HOME IMPROVEMENT	Andy Cadiff
ER	Hal Cooper
ALL MY CHILDREN (Recurring)	ABC-TV
FULL HOUSE	Joel Zwick
SISTERS	Kevin Inch
"ONCE A STRANGER"	Bev Foradi (HBO)

STAGE - N.Y.

WHITSUNTIDE	St. Clement's
COLONIAL DUDES	Manhattan Thtr. Club
HERE BE DRAGONS	St. Clement's
THE WEB	Playwrights Horizons
HOGWASH	Albee/Barr Unit
DREAM ETUDE	New Thtr. Workshop
WUZIZ!	Old Reliable

…plus approximately 38 other roles

STAGE - L.A. & REGIONAL

THE TIME OF YOUR LIFE	Arena Stage
PICK UP AX	The Actors Gang/L.A.
WAITING FOR LEFTY	Ensemble Studio Thtr.
YOU CAN'T TAKE IT WITH YOU	Penn State Thtr. Festival
OUR TOWN	Penn State Thtr. Festival
THE KNACK	Jersey.City State College
BREAKING THE CODE	Dante Ensemble/Atlanta

COMMERCIALS: Reel available on request

TRAINING: Wynn Handman, Stella Adler (Acting Technique), Harry Garland (Voice), Jerry Lines (Dance), Keith Johnston (Improv), Ed Hooks (Scene Study)

SPECIAL SKILLS: Ride motorcycle, juggler, competitive at most sports

Here are some helpful tips for creating your resume:

- Don't lie about your credits. It could come back to haunt you. You might one day find yourself sitting across the desk from the casting director who cast that made-up credit.
- Don't inflate what you did. If you worked as an extra on a movie, don't try to make it look like you had a speaking part.
- Never, ever put extra work on a resume.
- Don't put the dates of productions next to the credits. It only makes the person reading the resume start focusing on how old you are, or it gets them wondering why there aren't more recent dates on there. It is a lose-lose situation.
- Note that the sample resume I have included does not list the actor's specific roles. Instead, he mentions who the director was, what theater he did the play in, which network it ran on, and so on.
- When you have your resumes run off at the print shop, have them cut to the exact size of your photo, so they will fit on the back without overlapping the edges.
- Attach your resume to your photo with two staples at the top. No glue. No scotch tape.
- Don't list an age range. It is in the eye of the beholder anyway. Leave off any reference to age and let your photo speak for you.
- If you are freelancing, or if you don't have representation yet, be sure to include contact info on the resume. However, women might want to leave off the home address because you never know who might pull your photo out of a trash can somewhere.
- When mailing photos and resumes, don't bother putting cardboard in the envelope. It only adds weight and doesn't prevent damage anyway.
- Want to give the impression of recent activity? Leave off a couple of credits when you type up the resume, and then write them in on each copy. It leaves the impression that you've been so busy working that you haven't had time to type up a new resume. Everybody wants a winner, remember?
- If you don't have an agent's logo to put on your resume, get a personal name/logo for yourself and use it there. Wonderful and inexpensive work is being done these days in copy centers and print shops utilizing laser printers. You can put the same

logo on your stationery and note pads, creating an identity for yourself.

- If you are represented by an agent, you might want to consider printing your resume on the agent's office stationery.
- Note the "commercials" category on the sample resume. The actor typed in "reel available on request" instead of listing products. You can also write "conflicts on request," and you may want to list a few advertising agencies you have worked with. Never list products, however, because a campaign may be dead and still be carried on your resume, costing you possible auditions and jobs.

CHAPTER 13

Performers' Unions

Before there were performers' unions, there were two categories of actors: stars and everybody else. The stars were always well paid and coddled because they sold tickets. All the other players were considered to be interchangeable. If one didn't work out, there was another one behind the next tree. It was a classic case of supply outstripping demand, and it kept pay scales low while exploitation levels remained high.

Today we still have an imbalance in supply and demand but thanks to the unions, some dignity has been brought to the working, nonstar actor. Now we have acceptable wage scales, pension plans, health insurance, dental coverage, and safety standards on sets and stages. We get residuals when our performances are sold again and again on television.

There are three primary performers' unions with which you should be concerned.

Screen Actors Guild:
SAG's jurisdiction includes motion pictures, most prime-time television, most television commercials, most industrial/corporate films, and anything else that might be shot on film instead of videotape. Currently there are about 90,000 members of this important union.

American Federation of Television and Radio Artists:
AFTRA has jurisdiction over about 10 percent of the TV commercials, a hunk of the interactive media market, all radio commercials, all live television shows such as newscasts, all soap operas, some corporate films, and anything else that might be shot on

videotape instead of film. Currently, there are about 80,000 members.

Actors' Equity Association:
Equity covers live stage performances, period. It was the first union, the granddaddy, formed in 1913 by 112 actors who were braver than us all. Currently there are about 40,000 members, mostly in New York.

The time will surely come when SAG and AFTRA will be merged into a single union. It's long overdue. I won't be surprised to see the day when there will be a single union for all of the creative crafts, including directors, writers, and actors. Negotiations with producers get tougher each year. We don't negotiate our labor contracts with Sam Goldwyn anymore. Acting is now a small expense item to the honchos who live high up in the towers of their huge conglomerates. Artists must unite.

Until then, you'll have to deal with several different unions, and they all have different forms. SAG and Equity are national unions with branches around the country. When you pay your SAG dues they go to Hollywood, which then doles out money to support the various branches. AFTRA is actually a series of local unions joined together in a federation, so when you pay your AFTRA dues, you pay to your local. Then all the locals pitch some money into a pot to support a national office in New York and one in Hollywood. It's a pain in the neck, but be glad we have the unions at all, particularly in these very anti–labor union days.

HOW TO GET INTO THE UNIONS

In a nutshell, you'll be eligible to join the unions when you get cast in a production that is covered by a union contract. It works like this: The Taft–Hartley Act, passed by Congress in the late 1940s, set up the mechanism by which most people enter the unions. That act says that, if an employer (it might be a meat packer or a movie studio) has a union shop and wants to hire a person who is not in the union, then that person is allowed to work for thirty days under that union's jurisdiction without having to join the union; if the worker continues in the job for longer than thirty days, then he or she must join the union; if the person works the thirty days and doesn't get an offer to stay at work, then it is his or her option whether to join or not.

What this means is that, if a producer has signed an agreement with SAG (or AFTRA or AEA) allowing employment of union members, and he or she wants to hire an actor who is not yet in the union, then that actor must be allowed to join the union. the actor doesn't *have* to join if he or she doesn't want to until thirty days are up, but can if desired. In even plainer English, if you go to a commercial audition (or movie or stage play) and wind up with the job, you can take your contract to the union office and join up.

It is expensive to be a union member. The current fee to join Equity is $800, SAG costs $1,234, and AFTRA is $1,000. And once you are a member, you have to pay dues every six months, based on your earnings. Be glad you don't want to be a movie director. It costs over $5,000 to join the DGA.

I remember being terribly frustrated and defensive about my inability to get into the unions when I started out in New York. One of the first questions asked by every casting director and agent was "Are you in the unions?" I would mutter something about "not yet" and hope they wouldn't hold it against me. Then, one fine day I got cast, and all my union problems ended. I was in, a pro! I share this with you so you'll know you aren't alone. Nobody was born with a union card. They have to be earned. If you really want to pursue a career as a professional actor, you'll get into the unions, all of them. I guarantee it.

CHAPTER 14

The Internet and Digital Filmmaking

As Artonin Artaud observed, actors are athletes of the heart. Computers are the opposite of that. Actors are lovers, not geeks. We rejoice in verse, lingering sunsets, and curtain calls, not in HTML code. Romance and emotion evaporate when you reduce the world to zeros, ones, and gigabytes. It's just not conceivable that Romeo would have expressed his love for Juliet in an e-mail rather than from her moonlit garden or that Willy Loman could have lived a longer life if he had worked from a home-based dot-com business.

Actors have been late arrivals at the cyberspace party, it's true, but the more important point is that we are definitely here now. We are poised at the threshold of a moment in the evolution of the entertainment industry that is as exciting and meaningful as was the earliest days of television. The Internet—and its sister technology, digital video—is changing how actors make a living and express their art. As I write this, Screen Actors Guild and AFTRA members are walking picket lines across the United States, locked in a bitter labor strike against the advertising industry. One of the major issues on the negotiating table is the unions' demand for the first contract to cover Internet reuse of commercials. Predictions are that advertisers will soon be spending $5–20 billion each year on the Internet, and actors want to be fairly compensated for such exposure. Furthermore, when the matter of commercials' reuse is settled, the performing unions will shift focus to Internet reuse of movies and television shows. This is a big wheel rolling now, and it is not going to stop.

Programming of all sorts is going to the Internet, either as a primary or secondary destination, and all of the parties involved in production are grabbing for a piece of the pie. Industry trade papers *Hollywood Reporter* and *Daily Variety* are reporting Internet deals side by side with traditional studio deals. Web sites such as AtomFilms.com and iFilm.com are taking their place next to traditional brick-and-mortar theatrical exhibitors. Suddenly it has become newsworthy if a five-minute digital video receives 40,000 "hits." Talent agents and producers are interested in how many "downloads" a particular video has generated. The Neilsen company, long known for measuring audience size for television programs, now has a division devoted to measuring traffic on web sites. Two years ago, there was virtually none of this kind of thing to be found in the trade press. Industry excitement about the Internet is palpable, as if we were witnessing the first movie premiere on the moon. It is therefore essential that today's actor understand what is happening in this new environment. You need to be as comfortable in cyberspace as you are backstage in the theater green room. If you are to take advantage of the new tools available to you, you must have routine access to a computer and must know how to use it to log on to the Internet.

We have much to talk about. But first we need to agree on some ground rules.

GROUND RULES FOR THIS CHAPTER

The Internet has its own terminology, and I'm going to presume you are familiar with it. Most people in the United States under the age of twenty-five use a computer as easily as their kitchen toaster nowadays, but the older generations are still playing technological catch up. If abbreviations and terms such as "URL," "surfing," "e-mail," "database," "log on," "search engine," and "online" cause you to scratch your head and wrinkle your nose, I strongly recommend that you pick up a couple of the many primers about the Internet and computers. You can never go wrong with the "Dummies" line of books and, yes, there is one entitled "The Internet for Dummies" by John R. Levine, Carol Baroudi, and Margaret Levine Young. Amazon.com sells that one as well as an extensive line of similar titles. At the Amazon.com web site, try these search words: "new to Internet," "new to computers," "introduction to computers." It is not possible in the context of this brief chapter to comprehensively explain the basics of computers. To help out, I have added some of the most commonly used Internet and computer terms to the glossary at the end of this book, but when it comes to basic computer education, you're on your own.

DEFINITION: WEB SITES (URLS)

There is one Internet term that demands special mention and its own description because I'll be using it a lot in this chapter. The abbreviation is "URL," which stands for Uniform Resource Locator. URLs are actually web site addresses on the World Wide Web (www). Think of them as street addresses in a town, except that this town is in cyberspace. I will be referring to web sites, for instance, www.atomfilms.com or www.amazon.com. As is the case with people's telephone numbers and home addresses, things change, folks move around. A live URL today may be a "dead link" tomorrow. If you click on an Internet address that I've recommended and find that it is dead, do not despair. Most likely it has just moved down the cyberstreet. That's when you should open a good search engine, like Yahoo, and try a subject search. (You can think of a search engine as a kind of glorified telephone book, arranged by subject as well as name.) Indeed, one of the first skills you need to master on the Internet is how to conduct efficient searches. There are half a dozen really excellent search engines available, each of which operates in slightly different ways. For good introductory tutorials on search engines, plus an up-to-date list of them, try this web site: www.searchengine watch.com/facts/index.html.

AN ACTOR'S OVERVIEW OF THE INTERNET

Here are a few ways you will use the Internet:

1. You put your e-mail address on your resume and other promotional materials, right alongside your telephone number. Your fellow professionals as well as your mom have a new way to keep in touch with you.
2. Your agent arranges an audition for you at Paramount. Back in the horse-and-buggy days of the 1980s, you had to drive over to the studio or to your agent's office to pick up the sides. Now you can simply download them from a service such as ShowFax (www.showfax.com). Within moments of getting the call from your agent, you can be reading the script, gaining an advantage over the competition.

3. You have been cast in Shakespeare's *Richard III* and want to research the role. Today, instead of going to the library, you can log on while you're still in your pajamas. The Internet contains the equivalent of several libraries' worth of resources on virtually every subject imaginable, from Richard III (www.richard111.com/) to how to assemble a butterfly net (altern.org/ornithoptera/butnet.html.)

4. You've had some new photos taken and want your acting teacher to take a look at the proof sheets. You can wait until she returns from her much-deserved vacation in Italy, or you can scan the photos into the Internet, where they can be reviewed online. Your teacher checks her e-mail from a cyber-café in Florence, clicks on the link to your photos, and voilà! She renders her opinion long distance, no fuss, no muss.

5. You are feeling isolated and unappreciated and want to talk about things with other actors. Subscribe to the newsgroup alt.acting. A newsgroup is sort of like an office bulletin board, a place where people of similar interests can leave messages for one another, or for whomever passes by. If someone starts a new topic—known as a "thread"—then you can participate in the dialogue. Maybe you want to talk to other actors who have played Richard III. Post a "new message" to the news-group, give it a title like "Have you played Richard III?" and you're bound to attract correspondents.

6. You have saved up your money to see some plays and you want to know what is currently running in New York and London. No problem. Log on and start surfing. Lists of current productions in New York and London can be found at www.playbill.com. How about Chicago? Try www.chicago.il.org.

7. You are searching for a fresh monologue and you prefer something from a movie. Check out this web site: www.whysanity.net/monos.

8. You enjoy an actor's performance in a television show and want to know what other shows or films he or she has appeared in. Go to the Internet Movie Database (us.imdb.com) and type the name into the search engine there. I don't know how the IMDB accumulates the information presented on its web site, but the listings are impressive. I have checked my own name there and discovered accurate listings for many of my resume credits. By the way, IMDB also has sister sites for the U.K. and Italy.

The Internet is a repository of vast amounts of information, much of it changing on a daily basis. It is an environment, a communication device, and a new way of reaching out to touch somebody. In a word, the Internet is a pulsing, almost living, phenomenon of the late twentieth century, and it has become an essential tool for the actor of the twenty-first century.

A UNIVERSE OF WEB SITES

The World Wide Web is a spiderweb of interconnected Internet sites (URLs), one hyperlinked to the other. It works like this. Let's say you have clicked into the Internet Movie Data Base (us.imdb.com) and are reading about Laurence Olivier, who starred in and directed the 1954 movie of *Richard III.* You notice in his bio a reference to his second wife, Vivien Leigh, whose name on the computer screen is underlined and highlighted in blue. The highlighting indicates a hyperlink. Click on it, and you are immediately transported to her web site. There you discover that Vivien starred in the 1948 movie *Anna Karenina,* one of your favorites. You click on that and are transported to a site that contains a synopsis of *Anna Karenina,* a cast list, and links to a store where you can purchase the film itself, in DVD or VHS format. Isn't this fun?

As a first-hand example of how a web site can function, I will describe my own web site, www.edhooks.com. I use it to promote my workshops and books, to showcase myself as an actor, and as a bully pulpit for my views on acting and the entertainment industry. A visitor might find my web site in several ways. Someone who knows the precise address can simply tell the browser to go there. If you don't know my address but want to know about "acting classes san francisco" or "acting for animators," you can type those words into a search engine, and my name will turn up as a hyperlink. Regardless of how you arrive, you can click around within the site, moving from room to room (page to page actually, via hyperlink) in my cyberhouse. Over here is the library, down the hall is Ed's photo and resume, and up here is some information about Ed's classes. Those pictures on the wall are of Ed teaching classes. Have a question for Ed personally? No problem—each page of the site has instructions about how to "contact Ed Hooks." Click on that, and you can send Ed an e-mail.

My monthly Ed Hooks Newsletter is posted in my web site along with pages of career advice and links to other useful web sites. I even have a tie-in with Amazon (www.amazon.com), the world's largest bookstore. On my web site, you can read about acting books I recommend; if you want to purchase one of them, you can click on the title and be transported directly to Amazon. If you purchase the book that way, I earn a small commission from Amazon. You see how it works? A well-designed web site is a world in itself, self-sufficient and yet linked to the larger Internet world via hyperlinks and e-mail.

THE ENTERTAINMENT INDUSTRY ON THE WORLD WIDE WEB

When the average businessperson decides to build a web site, he or she thinks of it the way I do, as an expense item and a convenience, not a profit center. The big movie studios all have web sites, and it is clear as soon as you visit one of them that the sites are not in themselves intended to be profit centers. The studios are using the sites to promote their movies, maybe to sell a few T-shirts.

To some people, however, the Internet looks like the Yellow Brick Road. They see this wondrous new communication vehicle with its World Wide Web and millions of subscribers and tumble tub over tea kettle trying to figure ways to make money with it, designing business models that will get visitors to write checks and give out credit card numbers. But it's not as easy as it looks to make money this way, and so far the only consistently profitable Internet businesses are sex related.

When you log on to the Internet the first time, you are going to be faced with a lot of businesses selling goods and services to actors. Each of them will do their best to make you think they are successful and represent an inside track to Hollywood success. Keep in mind that things may not be what they seem. Anybody can build a dynamic web site, just as anybody can buy advertising space in the newspaper. The business model for many show-business-oriented enterprises on the Internet rests on the premise that a large number of actors can be persuaded to write checks. Caveat emptor.

CASTING IN CYBERSPACE

The most common and controversial actor-oriented Internet business is the Internet casting company. I wish I could give you a clear thumbs-up or thumbs-down on them, but I can't. In my opinion, these businesses are a mixed bag, and you should judge each one separately. In a nutshell, a cyber-casting company is a digital data-base of pictures and resumes. You pay a fee, usually $50–$100 per year, so you can put your photo and resume and maybe even a video of your song-and-dance routine in the company's database. You are motivated to pay the money by the hope that casting directors, talent agents, and directors will browse the database in search of actors. It is this last part that is the problem. In the real world of casting, nobody is much motivated to browse Internet actor data-bases unless they are being paid to do so. When money-paying acting jobs are at stake, casting directors contact talent agents, the folks who have a financial incentive (commissions) to represent the best available talent in the market. The major flaw in Internet databases is that the actors whose photos appear there are not screened for talent, only for check-writing ability.

A promotional strategy employed by some cyber-casting com-panies is to include high-profile casting directors in the company's core structure, either as owner-partners or as paid consultants. The casting director is put on the payroll, which is derived mainly from the money paid by the actors. In exchange, the casting director very publicly endorses the company. The advertising for the com-pany will say something like, "Joe Smith has cast the last five pic-tures for Steven Spielberg, and he thinks the XYZ Cyber-casting company is swell!" That type of thing certainly does appear to be an objective endorsement, doesn't it? You read that and you can reasonably conclude that Joe Smith is going to be hanging out at the database and that you just might have a crack at the next Steven Speilberg movie. But remember that Joe Smith is being *paid* for that endorsement! In a way, he is allowing himself to be used as bait to attract check-writing hopeful actors, the people who long for access to big and powerful casting directors like himself. It's a cynical business strategy aimed squarely at newcomer actors who don't know how the business actually functions.

There is, however, some counterbalancing good news on the cyber-casting scene. Competition among the companies has heat-ed up to the point that many of them have been forced to add extra services to attract check-writing actors, and the extra ser-vices alone might make subscription worthwhile. They might, for example, offer downloadable sides (scenes from movie or TV scripts); mailing lists of agents and casting directors; chat rooms where members can talk to other actors; online interviews with casting directors, agents, producers, and directors; general career advice; even discounts on photos and hair styling. All of these things are valuable tools and may be worth the money.

"WHO WANTS TO BE A MOVIE STAR?"

Recently, another mind-boggling variation of cyber-casting promotion has appeared in the Internet, and I'd like to talk about this one for a moment because it probably is a troubling harbinger of future promotions. In this deal, a cyber-casting company or movie-production company guarantees that, for a fee, hopeful actors will have access to a specific movie project. The actor pays to be included in a database that is to be reviewed by a casting director, or is invited to flat-out bid on a role. In other words, the stakes are being raised. Instead of selling the idea that *maybe* a casting director might see your photo if you pay to be in the database, this promotion *guarantees* it.

"Who Wants to be a Movie Star?" is the name of one such project, still in progress as I write this. Organized by a bunch of Hollywood entrepreneurs, an auction for roles was set up at Yahoo's Auction web site. (You'll find Yahoo Auction if you click onto the home page of Yahoo.) Aspiring actors (no experience required) are invited to bid on roles, and once the top bidders are "cast," the movie will be written for them, and produced. Exhibition at a film festival is guaranteed, as is release of the movie onto video. The high bid for lead roles in this yet-to-be-written movie is up to $16,000. Supporting roles are going for $5,000. Executive-producer billing is also up for sale, as are other behind-the-scenes titles. The Q&A page of the company's web site explains that one does not need training to be an actor. The promoters put it this way: "It seems that, more than in any other profession, the best training an actor can receive is on the job." And they cite James Cagney's famous line about how he plants his feet on the ground, looks the other actor in the eye, and "tells the truth." If that is all that acting amounted to, I for one would not have spent my life involved with it. Acting is an art form, like music and painting, something honorable to do in this world. Acting is not synonymous with stardom and, in fact, there is very little you can do if you want to become a star. A promotion like "Who Wants to be a Movie Star?" is demeaning to all true actors.

THE FUTURE OF CYBER-CASTING

It stands to reason that digital transmission of photos and videotaped performances has the potential for streamlining communication between agents and casting directors and for making the process more efficient. And certainly an actor's digital portfolio is going to be more environmentally friendly than the traditional headshot and lithograph. It is therefore safe to predict that, in time, the Internet will largely replace the old ways of doing things and will open up new points of contact between actors, agents, and casting directors. It is also safe to predict that, in time, humans will live on the moon. That doesn't mean that it makes good sense to start buying window seats on rocket ships today.

Once again, let's review the traditional procedure for casting:

1. Talent agents work for actors. They earn their money from commissions on acting jobs they arrange for their clients. Therefore, talent agents have a financial incentive to represent the best available talent in the market.
2. Casting directors work for producers. They are paid by producers to go out into the world and find actors to audition for whatever project is being cast. Though casting directors can theoretically pull in people from the local shopping mall for auditions, they will typically contact talent agents.

Screen Actors Guild emphatically argues that actors should never pay for auditions, and for good reason. There is an imbalance in supply and demand in the acting business. There are far more actors than there are acting jobs. Actors may be tempted to start writing checks if they honestly believe that doing so will result in auditions, which are always hard to get. The challenge facing casting directors and agents is to use the Internet in a way that fosters excellence in casting. If the casting process is being used to lure check-writing newbies to the Internet, then we have a problem.

I am a cockeyed optimist, and I believe that in time these matters will be worked out. The day you see talent agents and casting directors paying for access to the cyber databases, that is a good indication that actors would be smart to be included in the databases. Just because the Internet is a technological marvel, however, that does not mean that an extra step has been added to the casting process. Promotion for the cyber-casting web sites frequently implies that things have changed, that actors who want to be cast must be included in the databases. It is not so—not yet anyway.

When in doubt, remember this: If an acting job pays money, then it is virtually certain that talent agents will be in the equation somewhere. In other words, if you want to be paid to act, then what you need is an enthusiastic and well-connected talent agent. You do not need a presence on half a dozen actor databases.

"BEAM ME UP, SCOTTY!" (GET AN E-MAIL ADDRESS! BUILD A WEB SITE!)

Many actors take advantage of the free e-mail service offered by Yahoo (www.yahoo.com) or Microsoft (www.hotmail.com). These companies figure that if they give you a free e-mail address, you'll hang around their web sites a lot, where you can be exposed to online advertising. It's a logical business proposition, and it is hard to beat the price. My wish for you, however, is that you spring for the bucks and get a paid e-mail address from one of the many Internet Service Providers (ISPs). Earthlink (www.earthlink.net), for example, is a top-drawer ISP that charges $20 or so per month for service, but you can be certain that your e-mail will get to you efficiently, which is something you cannot presume with the free e-mail services because they are hosting huge numbers of accounts. There are many thousands of ISPs available in the United States. Go to Yahoo and type "ISP" into the search engine, and you'll be directed to the ISPs in your area. There is also a web site (thelist.internet.com) where you can search for ISPs by your area code.

DEVELOPING A WEB SITE

There are two steps involved in developing your own web site. First you have to build it, and then you have to find a place in cyberspace to put it. If you are the adventurous sort, you can build your own web site by using off-the-shelf software like Adobe Pagemill, Front Page 2000, or HomePage 3.0. The software will cost you about $80–$125, and if you are as slow at these things as I am, it will take you a week or so of solid effort to get the site built. It's sort of like constructing a ship in a bottle. Some folks like to do it, and others don't. I'm one of those people who would rather hire someone to do it for me, but maybe you're one who likes to do it yourself. Fortunately there are many talented folk who really enjoy building web sites, and you should be able to hire one of them for a reasonable amount of money. Maybe you can even work out a trade of some kind with a friend who is good at it.

Once you get your site built, you have to put it somewhere. Most ISPs will host web sites for a small fee. My ISP is Best.com, a division of Vario, and they give me 25 megabytes of space for my web site at no addtional charge. I pay $35 per month for my e-mail, and Best hosts my site for free. That's a lot of bang for the buck.

DIGITAL VIDEO

Digital video (DV) is special because anything that is recorded on it is already in computer language. A movie shot on celluloid has to be transferred and digitized in an expensive laboratory process before it can be edited digitally. The DV image has already been rendered into zeros and ones. What this means is that movies shot on DV can be imported into a computer for editing and then painlessly uploaded into the Internet, where it can be downloaded by computer users all over the world.

In a nutshell, DV has made everybody and their Uncle Louie into potential movie makers. For a remarkably reasonable price (approximately $10,000 at this writing), you can purchase everything you need to make a bargain-basement DV movie, including camera, computer, and software. And given how easy it is to build your own web site, it is then possible to upload your movie into your site, where friends, family, and patrons can view it. The movie *Blair Witch Project* started it all. Released in 1999, this movie had a total budget of under $40,000, was shot by first-time movie makers, and has grossed $140 million dollars. It is an understatement to say that *Blair Witch Project* captured the attention of Hollywood studio execs. It used to be that the Hollywood system didn't touch movies with budgets of less than $15 million. Now you can find almost daily reports in the trade papers of movies with budgets in the $600,000 range, and DV is the key.

DV has hastened the union of television and computers, and it is transforming the way business is done in Hollywood. There are DV film festivals, DV magazines, DV workshops in all the major film schools. Now a producer who is hoping to make a megamillion-dollar-budget movie may well spend a few thousand on a DV preview showcase. The short film may find its way to one of the proliferating multiplex web sites such as Next Wave Films (www.nextwavefilms.com) or iFilm.com. If enough people download it and like it, Hollywood execs are more likely to start writing checks for a full-tilt feature film.

These cyberspace multiplexes are a fascination in themselves. Right now they mainly show little five- and ten-minute movies, and much of it is animation. This is going to expand because more and more people are buying computers and going online, and the computers they are buying have umpteen times the processing power that computers had eight or nine years ago. Also, the way data is downloaded is getting faster. The more powerful the computer, the faster the download time, the more complex and detailed will be the films exhibited in cyberspace. Take a few minutes and visit Atom Films (www.atomfilms.com) if you want to take a peek into the future.

There is currently a gusher of five- and ten-minute DV films in production. People who were previously locked out of the moviemaking process are going crazy, shooting DV on every street corner. The learning curve being what it is, most of these projects probably won't amount to much, but there is no denying the excitement in the air.

This development in DV is impacting on actors in several ways:

1. With more films being shot, there are more roles to be had. DV is creating more opportunities to act.
2. Actors are beginning to showcase themselves on DV, with clips of their work. This is a brand new tool for promotion, taking its place alongside the headshot and resume.
3. Some television shows are being simultaneously viewed on the Internet, a situation that would not exist were it not for DV. What this means is that actors are going to be getting paid more. Work that is recorded for television may very well show up on the Internet, and that means more money.
4. Audiences are becoming global. The reach of the performance is being extended beyond national borders. A DV movie shot in San Francisco can be downloaded in Tokyo and Johannesburg.
5. DV does not physically deteriorate and fade the way celluloid does. This means that work shot on DV today will be around fifty years from now, looking as fresh as it did the day it was recorded.

When the Big Boys embrace a new technology, you can be certain it has arrived to stay. George Lucas has announced that the live-action sequences of the next *Star Wars* movie will be shot on DV.

At the time of this writing, a feature-length DV movie entitled *Time Code*, directed by Mike Figgis *(Leaving Las Vegas)*, is playing in theaters across America. Spike Lee's upcoming movie *Bamboozled* is going to be shot on DV. Simon Beaufoy, the scriptwriter of the hit movie *The Full Monty*, is the chief writer for the digital episodic film *Running Time*, which airs over the web site www.itsyourmovie.com.

INTERNET MULTIPLEX AND PRODUCTION SITES

www.atomfilms.com
www.ifilm.com
www.honkworm.com
www.itsyourmovie.com
www.mediatrip.com
www.nextwavefilms.com
www.reelshort.com
www.neurotrash.com
www.sputnik7.com

DIGITAL FILM FESTIVALS

There are now film festivals devoted to the digital revolution. While you're browsing the Internet, check these out:

www.hollywoodnet.com Hollywood Digital Film Festival
www.leofest.com This festival is run by actor Leonardo DiCaprio!
www.pop.com POPFEST
www.resfest.com
www.zdnet.com/yil/filmfest/homepage/homepage.html Yahoo Internet Life Online Film Festival

ENTERTAINMENT INDUSTRY RESOURCES

The following list of Internet references is intended only to get you started. Once you begin surfing from one site to another, you will quickly develop your own list.

www.thegrid.net/virg ACTING-PRO, a list-serve for actors.
www.actorsequity.org Actors' Equity Association.
www.actorsite.com Showbiz portal, based in Hollywood. Lots of good links.
www.aftra.org American Federation of Television and Radio Artists (AFTRA).

Alt.acting Newsgroup.

americantheater.about.com/arts/americantheater/mbody.htm This site is full of fun theater stuff.

www.backstage.com Backstage West—DramaLogue.

www.Bartleby.com Shakespeare's complete works.

www.breakdownservices.com Breakdown Services.

www.canadianactor.com Canadian Actor Online. Many useful Canadian links.

www.caryn.com/biz Hollywood actress Caryn Shalita runs this site. Lots of good links.

www.castingworkbook.com Casting Work Book (Canada).

www.castnet.com CastNet.

www.dga.org/magazine Directors Guild of America magazine. Good interviews with important film people.

www.dramabookshop.com Drama Book Shop (New York).

www.dramatists.com Dramatists Play Service. Publishes acting editions of plays.

www.hollywoodreporter.com Hollywood Reporter.

us.imdb.com Internet Movie Database.

www.oscars.org Academy of Motion Picture Arts and Sciences. These are the Academy Awards people, and they publish the Player's Directory.

www.playbill.com Playbill On Line. All about the Broadway theater scene.

www.playersdirectory.com/index.html Player's Directory (Hollywood).

www.resmag.com RES, the magazine of digital filmmaking.

www.sag.org Screen Actors Guild.

www.samuelfrench.com Samuel French, Inc. Publishes acting editions of plays.

www.showfax.com ShowFAX.

www.simon.dunmore.btinternet.co.uk British director, teacher, and author Simon Dunmore runs this useful portal for actors who want to work in the United Kingdom. Simon also is the author of *An Actor's Guide to Getting Work* (A & C Black, 2001).

www.tcg.org Theatre Communications Group, organization of U.S. regional theaters. Publishes *American Theatre* magazine.

www.theatrebayarea.org Theatre Bay Area (San Francisco).

www.TVIndustry.com TV Industry news.

www.variety.com Daily Variety.

CHAPTER 15

"What Do *You* Think?" Questions and Opinions

I n no particular order, and with no particular categorization, I offer the following commonly asked questions, along with my opinions.

Is there anything special I should be doing as a minority performer?
Probably. Though we've come a long way since the fifties, we have miles to go before we sleep. According to a 1999 SAG report, only 3.5 percent of roles cast are going to Latinos; Native Americans get only .2 percent, and Asian Pacific performers get 2.1 percent. All of the unions have Affirmative Action programs, in which producers are urged to cast minorities, even given incentives to do so. You might consider contacting a local union office to see if you can add your voice to the chorus. Also, if you ask around in the theatrical community, you'll probably discover independent associations of performers who have banded together to pepper casting directors and producers with photos and mailings on an organized basis.

How do I stay in touch with my agent?
Drop by now and then. Show off your new haircut, or bring in a box of fortune cookies. Particularly early on in your relationship, you want to be visible, not just a name on a list. Telephone calls are pretty much a waste of time, even though I know some agents who encourage their clients to "check in" this way. I think they tell you that to keep you from dropping by. Your agent is busy, or should be, and you don't want to monopolize his or her time, so use good judgment if you visit the office. Drop by, say hi, and leave. If you are there for fifteen minutes, that's too long.

What kind of training should I have? How can I find good instructors?
The answer to the first part is that you should have as broad a lib-
eral arts education as possible. There is no such thing as a good
dumb actor. Read deeply in history, philosophy, and literature. I
tell my acting students that I would rather see them reading the
New York Times or a novel by Hemingway than another tome on
acting technique. Actors are artists and should have something to
say. Get a university education if you can. If my daughter wanted
to be an actress, I would advise her to complete college and then
try to get into a place like Julliard or the NYU Tisch School of
Drama for intense, broad-based training in acting skills.

Once in the field, by all means find a good professional scene-
study workshop, and stay in it. That is where you can stretch, trying roles you might otherwise not be cast in. Singing and dancing
classes are good, as are improv workshops. If you have never
acted in commercials, then a commercial-auditioning workshop is
a must. At minimum, you need to know where to stand and how
to relate to the camera and use cue cards. As for "film acting"
classes, Hollywood is full of them, and they are fine just as long
as you realize that you are studying camera technique and not
acting technique. If you have never had any acting training, a
straightforward scene-study workshop that does not employ a
camera is a far better place to be than "film acting" class.
Improvisational training is wonderful. I recommend training that
includes the theories of Keith Johnstone (author of *Impro*).

To find good instructors, ask fellow actors whom they like. As
with the poll you did when searching for photographers, you'll
hear the same names pop up again and again. Most legitimate
teachers will permit you to audit their classes, and that is the best
thing to do. Indeed, if a teacher will not allow auditors, that
should be seen as a red flag.

One word of caution to those who live in cities other than New
York and Hollywood: it is not uncommon to find yourself sitting
across the desk from a talent agent who also owns and operates
an acting school. Some of these schools may be excellent, but
tread carefully. Watch out for agents who want to "develop" you
at their school or who offer a quid pro quo. ("I'll represent you if
you enroll in the classes we offer.") It just might be the case that
you are looking at a person who is more in the school business
than the agenting business and is using the agent aspect to lure
prospective students. Though good training is a critical part of

becoming a professional actor, when you are interviewing with agents, you should be looking for representation, not classes. It is one thing for agents to advise you to go get some acting training and to perhaps suggest some classes to check out, but it is quite another if they themselves are offering a six-month or one-year "comprehensive program of acting training." Proceed with care.

Finally, I pass along advice that was given to me once by a very fine actor, Conrad Bain. At a time when I was considering leaving the business for earnest work, he said to me, "For every actor I have known who has not made it because he hasn't had the big break, I can name ten who have had the big break and weren't ready for it." So, whatever you do, stay in training. Be ready.

Should I do extra work?

You'll get conflicting advice on this. Extra work in commercials pays more than extra work in movies. If you are in Hollywood and you aspire to a big acting career, I advise that you not do much extra work. If you are in New York, maybe. Tradition in New York is different than in L.A. In New York, actors might work as extras for a few dollars of income. In L.A., there are professional extras, people who really do not aspire to lead roles at all. If you live anywhere else, follow local dictates. Regardless of where you do extra work, you must not put it on your resume. Extra work is not considered to be acting.

The main problem with extra work is that a steady diet of it can take a toll on your ego. I honestly believe that one of the keys to getting cast is the conviction that you *should* be cast, that you are good enough to carry a lead role, and it's hard to feel that way about yourself if you are working on a set where you are a coat size. Also, there is no ladder up that begins with doing extra work. In the entertainment industry, there are actors and there are extras, and never the twain shall meet.

Should I move to Los Angeles? New York?

These two cities certainly dominate the entertainment industry today, and if you are serious about making a career of it, you should consider a move. Which place is better? I've lived in both, and my perception is that New York is a story about the legitimate theater and art; Hollywood is a story about movies, TV, and money. Wherever you go, I urge you not to do it halfheartedly. Make the move, and make a serious commitment. At minimum, give it a good three- to five-year effort.

If you are just starting on your career, however, you can build a handsome resume right where you are, and my advice is to do that before going to either New York or Hollywood. Act in plays and student films at local colleges. Do some corporate films. You'll be in a better place if you already have a resume when you make the big move.

How about being a bi-city actor, working two cities at once?
I have done this for several years, dividing my time between Los Angeles and San Francisco, and I am here to attest to how difficult it can be. The primary obstacle is that employers in both cities want to deal with you as local talent. Agents are not much interested in representing long-distance clients. If you are cast in a role in Hollywood, and if you are living three hundred miles away, the producer will have to pay your travel, per diem, hotel expenses, and so forth. That's a deal killer and will cost you the job. Therefore, if you want to try this trick, you need to establish bases in both cities, complete with mailing addresses and local telephone numbers. (Voice mail works fine for this purpose.)

Are casting director showcases worthwhile?
These functions are among the most controversial in the industry. Hollywood and New York are chock full of them. Check the trade papers for dates and times. The casting director showcase usually involves actors in a group who read with or for a casting director. Then the casting director gives you pointers on audition technique. The problem is that actors should not have to pay for auditions, and some of the showcases make it seem like that is precisely what you are doing. Even if you call them workshops or classes, how can you avoid the audition aspect? Let's be honest: At least in part you are paying a fee to meet that casting director, and you are hoping you will get discovered, right? The truth is that very few people actually score jobs from these functions because casting directors are going to call talent agents when they are casting jobs that pay money.

As you can tell, I'm not a fan of casting director workshops or showcases and generally recommend against them. However, I understand I am fighting City Hall. If you are bound and determined to showcase in this fashion, then at least do it with your eyes wide open. Make sure that your audition techniques are already top drawer, absolutely competitive, before doing the showcases. Get some training, and *then* showcase. That way, you'll be getting the biggest bang for the buck.

How do I avoid being typecast? Won't it ruin my career?
You have to have a career to ruin first. The truth is that it is desirable to be typed at the start of your career. At least that way they know what to do with you. My advice is to take any work you can get and worry about shaping your career later.

Casting notices in the trade papers always specify
"no calls and no visits." Is that true?
From the casting director's perspective, yes. From your perspective, maybe. If you believe you are right for a role, I advocate doing everything in your power to be auditioned for it. If they don't respond to a mailing quickly, then call or visit. As long as you are friendly and professional about it, no one can fault you for trying to sell your services.

Any suggestions about how to support myself
while hunting for acting work?
A book could be written about the strange and wonderful ways in which actors have supported themselves while "between engagements." The problem is that you rarely get more than twenty-four hours notice of auditions, and usually it is less than that. It is common to get a call at 10:30 A.M. for a 2:30 P.M. audition. In other words, you have to be able to spin on a dime. This can be a major stumbling block for people who are already entrenched in good-paying real-world jobs when they want to break into show business.

Should I quit my job, or should I just call in sick when I get an audition?
Conventional jobs for Fortune 500 companies usually aren't the kind that you can pop in and out of when that exciting reading for a Pampers commercial suddenly comes up. Most mainstream employers simply aren't sensitive to the artistic urge, yet you absolutely must be available for auditions when they happen because the agents and casting directors will quickly stop calling you if you can't get there. I worked for a year or so as a desk clerk in a women's hotel in New York, midnight until seven in the morning, just so I could have my days free. The aspiring actor who is working at Macy's has become almost a joke. Everybody,

it seems, has worked there at one time or another. Waiting tables and parking cars is good. The best thing would be to find a way to be self-employed so you have more control over your hours, but if that isn't possible, look at seasonal jobs, food-service jobs such as catering, night-shift employment, temp jobs. A lot of actors work commission-only sales jobs because they can call their hours their own.

How do I get my child into commercials/TV/movies?
All parents believe that their kids have star quality, and sometimes this is even true. But the pathway into the business for children is rocky indeed. I don't think that very young children, say under about ten years of age, profit much from acting classes or modeling schools. Children are intuitive and naturally playful. Some are born performers and some are shy. If your child is outgoing and doesn't mind being under hot lights and working very closely with strangers (in commercials, strangers will be playing Mommy and Daddy), then go ahead and take a few snapshots and send them to talent agents in your city who handle children. You can obtain the list of these agents from the Screen Actors Guild. You don't need 8x10 headshots yet, just a few good snapshots. If the agents like the child's look, you'll be invited in for an interview. If that works out, the agent may suggest you spring for headshots. The problem is, of course, that children physically change so rapidly that headshots are out of date almost as soon as you get them. Commercials, by the way, are the easiest road into movies and TV shows for children. Start there.

Can I deduct my acting expenses from my income tax?
You should check with your accountant on this one, but the short answer is that, if you have income from acting, then you can deduct the expenses you accumulated in order to generate that income. Once you are working in the biz, the union dues, acting classes, photos, and resumes are all deductible. So is the cost of going to a movie. Actors live in an upside down world. What is entertainment for most normal humans is education for us, and is therefore deductible.

What about overexposure in commercials?
You should be so lucky.

Conclusion

Say this out loud right now: "I am an actor."

How did it feel? Odd? *Are* you an actor? Or do you hope to be one someday? Just because you may not have earned a single dime from acting yet does not mean that you are not an actor. They say that Picasso painted more than 1,000 paintings before he ever sold one. Was he any more an artist at number 1,000 than he was at 999? Was Vincent Van Gogh less of an artist because he never sold any?

Artistry is a state of mind, a determination to communicate, and it is important for you to acknowledge your art. You need not torture yourself for not having worked as much as you think you should have. It only means you are normal.

In the same year that Babe Ruth set the record for the most home runs hit, he also held the record for the most strike-outs.

Remember that.

Appendix: Union Offices

AFTRA LOCALS

ARIZONA
1616 East Indian School Road, #330
Phoenix, AZ 85016
(602) 265-2712
(602) 264-7571 fax

CALIFORNIA
4831 East Shields Avenue, Suite 32
Fresno, CA 93724
(209) 252-1655
(209) 252-1655 fax

5757 Wilshire Boulevard, 9th floor
Los Angeles, CA 90036
(323) 634-8100
(323) 634-8246 fax

7867 Convoy Court, Suite 307
San Diego, CA 92111-1214
(858) 278-7695
(858) 278-2505 fax

235 Pine Street, 11th Floor
San Francisco, CA 94104
(415) 391-7510
(415) 391-1108 fax

c/o 1261 El Sur Way
Sacramento, CA 95864
(916) 925-0443
(916) 483-7145 fax

COLORADO
950 South Cherry Street, #502
Denver, CO 80222
(303) 757-6226
(303) 757-1769 fax

FLORIDA
20401 N.W. 2nd Avenue, #102
Miami, FL 33169
(305) 652-4824
(305) 652-4846
(305) 652-2885 fax

GEORGIA
455 East Paces Ferry Road, NE, Suite 334
Atlanta, GA 30305
(404) 239-0131
(404) 239-0137 fax

HAWAII
949 Kapiolani Boulevard,
Suite #105
Honolulu, HI 96814
(808) 596-0388
(808) 593-2636 fax

ILLINOIS
One East Erie,
Suite 650
Chicago, IL 60611
(312) 573-8081
(312) 573-0318 fax

INDIANA
See TRI-STATE

KENTUCKY
See TRI-STATE

LOUISIANA
2400 Augusta Drive,
Suite 264
Houston, Texas 77057
(713) 972-1806
(713) 780-0261 fax

MARYLAND
4340 East West Highway,
#204
Bethesda, MD 20814
(301) 657-2560
(301) 656-3615 fax

MASSACHUSETTS
11 Beacon Street, #512
Boston, MA 02108
(617) 742-2688
(617) 742-4904 fax

MICHIGAN
27770 Franklin Road
Southfield, MI 48034
(248) 355-3105
(248) 355-2879 fax

Detroit Broadcast Division
260 Madison Avenue, 7th floor
New York, NY 10016
(212) 532-0800
(212) 532-2242 fax

MINNESOTA
708 North First Street
Suite 333, Itasca Bldg.
Minneapolis, MN 55401
(612) 371-9120
(612) 371-9119 fax

MISSOURI
P.O. Box 32167
4000 Baltimore, 2nd floor
Kansas City, MO 64111
(816) 753-4557
(816) 753-1234 fax

1310 Papin, Suite 103
St. Louis, MO 63103
(314) 231-8410
(314) 231-8412 fax

NEBRASKA
3000 Farnham Street, Suite 3
East Omaha, NE 68131
(402) 346-8384

NEW YORK
c/o WGY-AM/WRVE-FM
1 Washington Square
Albany, NY 11205
(518) 452-4800

c/o WIVB-TV
2077 Elmwood Avenue
Buffalo, NY 14207
(716) 879-4985

260 Madison Avenue,
7th floor
New York, NY 10016
(212) 532-0800
(212) 545-1238 fax

87 Fairlea Drive
Rochester, NY 14622
(716) 467-7982

170 Ray Avenue
Schenectady, NY 12304
(518) 374-5915

c/o WRGB-TV
1400 Balltown Road
Schenectady, NY 12309
(518) 346-6666
(518) 346-6249 fax

OHIO
1030 Euclid Avenue,
Suite 429
Cleveland, OH 44115-1504
(216) 781-2255
(216) 781-2257 fax
See also TRI-STATE

OREGON
3030 S.W. Moody,
Suite #104
Portland, OR 97201
(503) 279-9600
(503) 279-9603 fax

PENNSYLVANIA
230 South Broad Street,
Suite 500
Philadelphia, PA 19102-1229
(215) 732-0507
(215) 732-0086 fax

625 Stanwix Street
Pittsburgh, PA 15222
(412) 281-6767
(412) 281-2444

TENNESSEE
P.O. Box 121087
1108 17th Avenue South
Nashville, TN 37212
(615) 327-2944
(615) 329-2803 fax

TEXAS
6060 N. Central Expressway
Suite 302, L.B. 604
Dallas, TX 75206
(214) 363-8300
(214) 363-5386 fax

2400 Augusta, #264
Houston, TX 77057
(713) 972-1806
(713) 780-0261 fax

TRI-STATE
(includes Cincinnati,
Columbus, and Dayton, OH;
Indianapolis, IN;
Louisville, KY)
128 East 6th Street, #802
Cincinnati, OH 45202
(513) 579-8668
(513) 579-1617 fax

WASHINGTON
601 Valley Street, #100
Seattle, WA 98109
(206) 282-2506
(206) 282-7073 fax

WASHINGTON, D.C.
See MARYLAND

ACTORS' EQUITY ASSOCIATION

NATIONAL OFFICE
165 West 46th Street,
15th Floor
New York, NY 10036
(212) 869-8530
(212) 719-9815 fax

BRANCH OFFICES

5757 Wilshire Boulevard,
Suite One
Los Angeles, CA 90036
(323) 634-1750
(323) 634-1777 fax

235 Pine Street, Suite 1200
San Francisco, CA 94104
(415) 391-3838
(415) 391-0102 fax

10319 Orangewood Boulevard
Orlando, FL 32821
(407) 345-8600
(407) 345-1522 fax

203 North Wabash Avenue,
Suite 1700
Chicago, IL 60601
(312) 641-0393

(312) 641-6365 fax

SCREEN ACTORS GUILD

NATIONAL HEADQUARTERS
5757 Wilshire Boulevard
Los Angeles, CA 90036-3600
(323) 954-1600

BRANCH OFFICES

ALABAMA
See FLORIDA

ARIZONA
1616 E. Indian School Road,
Suite 330
Phoenix, AZ 85016
(602) 265-2712
(602) 264-7571 fax

ARKANSAS
See FLORIDA

CALIFORNIA
7867 Convoy Court, Suite 307
San Diego, CA 92111-1214
(619) 278-7695
(619) 278-2505 fax

235 Pine Street, 11th floor
San Francisco, CA 94104
(415) 391-7510
(415) 391-1108 fax

COLORADO
950 South Cherry Street, Suite 502
Denver, CO 80222
(800) 527-7517 or (303) 757-6226
(303) 757-1769 fax

FLORIDA
7300 North Kendall Drive,
Suite #620
Miami, FL 33156-7840
(305) 670-7677
(305) 670-1813 fax

646 West Colonial Drive
Orlando, FL 32804-7342
(407) 649-3100
(407) 649-7222 fax

GEORGIA
455 E. Paces Ferry Road NE,
Suite 334
Atlanta, GA 30305
(404) 239-0131
(404) 239-0137 fax

HAWAII
949 Kapiolani Blvd., #105
Honolulu, HI 96814
(808) 538-0388
(808) 593-2636 fax

ILLINOIS
1 East Erie, Suite #650
Chicago, IL 60611
(312) 573-8081
(312) 573-0318 fax

LOUISIANA
See FLORIDA

MARYLAND
4340 East West Highway,
Suite 204
Bethesda, MD 20814
(301) 657-2560
(301) 656-3615 fax

MASSACHUSETTS
11 Beacon Street,
Room 515
Boston, MA 02108
(617) 742-2688
(617) 742-4904 fax

MICHIGAN
27770 Franklin Road
Southfield, MI 48034-2352
(248) 355-3105
(248) 355-2879 fax

MINNESOTA
708 North 1st Street,
Suite #333
Minneapolis, MN 55401
(612) 371-9120
(612) 371-9119 fax

MISSISSIPPI
See FLORIDA

MISSOURI
1310 Papin Street,
Suite #1006
St. Louis, MO 63103
(314) 231-8410
(314) 231-8412 fax

NEVADA
980 Paradise Road,
Suite #162
Las Vegas, NV 89109
(702) 737-8818
(702) 737-8851 fax

NEW MEXICO
See COLORADO

NEW YORK
1515 Broadway, 44th Floor
New York, NY 10036
(212) 944-1030
(212) 944-6774 fax

NORTH CAROLINA
311 North Second Street, Suite 2
Wilmington, NC 28401
(910) 762-1889
(910) 762-0881 fax

OHIO
1030 Euclid Avenue,
Suite #429
Cleveland, OH 44115
(216) 579-9305
(216) 781-2257 fax

OREGON
3030 S.W. Moody, Suite #104
Portland, OR 97201
(503) 279-9600
(503) 279-9603 fax

PENNSYLVANIA
230 South Broad Street,
10th floor
Philadelphia, PA 19102
(215) 545-3150
(215) 732-0086 fax

PUERTO RICO
530 Ponce de Leon Avenue,
Suite #312
San Juan, PR 00901
(787) 289-7832
(787) 289-8732 fax

SOUTH CAROLINA
See FLORIDA

TENNESSEE
P.O. Box 121087
Nashville, TN 37212
(615) 327-2944
(615) 329-2803 fax

TEXAS
6060 N. Central Expressway
Suite 302, LB 604
Dallas, Texas 75206
(214) 363-8300
(214) 363-5386 fax

2400 Augusta Drive,
#264
Houston, TX 77057
(713) 972-1806
(713) 780-0261 fax

UTAH
See COLORADO

WASHINGTON
601 Valley Street, Suite 100
Seattle, WA 98109
(206) 270-0493
(206) 282-7073 fax

WASHINGTON, D.C.
See MARYLAND

WEST VIRGINIA
See FLORIDA

Glossary

Academy Players Directory Published by the Academy of Motion Picture Arts and Science and known these days simply as the Players Directory, this telephone-book-sized volume contains contact info on actors in Hollywood.

Actors' Equity Association AEA. The union that covers the legitimate stage only, no film or TV. Both actors and stage managers are members.

A.D. Short for Assistant Director. On a film or set there is usually a First A.D. and one or more Second A.D.s. They keep things organized, tell the extras which way to move, and so forth. In general terms, the A.D. in films is equivalent to a **stage manager** in theater except that an A.D. is usually serious about becoming an actual director. It is a stepping-stone position. A First A.D. outranks a Second A.D.

ad agency The creative nerve center of commercials. The concepts originate here, and the actual production is subcontracted to a **production house.**

ADR Abbreviation for Automatic Dialogue Replacement. Now that computers have entered the picture, this is the new name for looping.

AFTRA Another performers' union. The American Federation of TV and Radio Artists covers all radio, all live TV, most TV shows recorded on videotape (such as game shows, variety shows, and soap operas), as well as most corporate films.

agent The actor's representative in the marketplace. The distinction to keep in mind is that some agents are **franchised** and some are not. Those that are have been approved by the unions to represent union talent. Even if you aren't in the union, you need a franchised agent. They collect 10 percent of your earnings as their fee. Not to be confused with **manager.**

AGMA Associated Guild of Musical Artists. One of the affiliated performers' unions.

AGVA Associated Guild of Variety Artists. Another of the affiliated performers' unions.

animatic A kind of quasi-commercial that ad agencies sometimes employ to show a client the general idea of a campaign. They shoot a series of stills with a regular SLR camera and then videotape them so that, when the tape is replayed, there is a feeling of animation. If the client likes the animatic, they might go ahead and make a full production spot.

ANNCR OR V/O Announcer or Voice Over. Usually refers to an off-camera performer who records his or her part in a sound studio. Later it is mechanically edited into the film. You see these abbreviations a lot in commercial scripts. V/O could also refer to what we hear while a picture of something else is on the screen. A commercial might start out with a performer O/C and then, as we pan to a product shot, we still hear the performer talking. In the script that would be indicated as: "Performer V/O."

apron On a proscenium stage, this is the frontal lip of the stage, the part closest to the audience.

art director The person who designs sets, usually on commercials.

ATA Association of Talent Agents.

availability In commercials, after final auditions, the producer may specify a potential time span for the shoot and ask for your "availability." It means that, if you get an offer for another job during that time, you should tell the producer so he or she can book you first if desired. It is all a courtesy and has no legal status at all. It doesn't mean you are going to get paid.

best boy On film sets, the best boy is an assistant to the **gaffer** and helps handle all the equipment. Has nothing to do with age.

blue sky A film term that involves camera and editing tricks.

They might shoot an actual burning building, for example, and then later film the firemen running up and down a ladder in a parking lot somewhere with the "blue sky" behind them. Then, in the editing room, the two shots are put together to make it seem as if the firemen were actually at the site of the fire.

book As in "Could I see your book, Bob?" Otherwise known as a portfolio, all models carry these around as they go to interviews. Actors who have impressive collections of stills from past shows ("This is me as Portia. . . .") sometimes like to have a book, but it certainly is not necessary.

booking As in "You have a booking, Roberta." You only hear this term in commercials and modeling, never in theater. It means you got the job. If they cancel after this, you still get a session fee.

boom An overhead microphone, usually held on a long pole.

brick and mortar A store in the real world, something made out of actual building materials, as opposed to a store on the Internet, which is made out of nothing.

callback They saw the immediate world at the first audition and have narrowed down the field to a few promising candidates, of which you are one. The callback is a second, third, or fourth audition.

call sheet On a film or TV show, this is prepared daily by the production office and is a handy thing to have. Among other info, it contains a list of the actors who are working the next day and tells what their call times are. You can get one from the A.D.

call time The time you are supposed to report to the set on a film, TV show, or commercial. When you get there, check in with the A.D.

camera left The actor's right when facing the camera. Just remember, camera left is the opposite of **stage left.** Camera left is from the cameraperson's perspective; stage left is from the actor's perspective.

camera right The actor's left when facing the camera.

card A term you'll hear when your agent is negotiating your billing on a film or TV show. Your name might appear alone on the screen ("separate card") or with others ("shared card").

casting director Person who has the job of finding appropriate actors to audition for the roles; works for the producer.

client The company that pays the bills in commercials. If you are doing a spot for Pampers, then Proctor & Gamble is the client.

commission A percentage of a performers earnings paid to agents or managers for services rendered.

composite A two-sided composition of photos used almost exclusively by actors who do commercials. Usually the front displays a headshot, and the reverse contains four or five situational shots that show how you can be cast. Not to be confused with a **headshot** or a **Zed card.**

conflicts As in, "Do you have any conflicts with Pepsi, Bob?" Union rules say that you can't have two commercials for the same kind of product running at the same time. You can't have a Pepsi and a Coke spot simultaneously. If you get caught with conflicting products on the air, you can get sued for production costs. It's not worth it.

cross Definitely not a religious term. It means that the actor is supposed to cross from one place to another on the set. As in, "You'll make your cross on your next line, Roberta."

CSA Casting Society of America.

cue The line immediately before yours. A cue can also be non-verbal. "Your cue is when the phone rings, Bob."

cue card Used in commercial auditions, this is a piece of white posterboard on which the casting director writes the copy with a magic marker and puts it on a stand next to the camera so you can refer to it instead of having to hold the script in your hand. SAG requires cue cards at auditions.

database This is a computer term. If you have a computerized list of, say, all the high schools in your city, that's a database.

day-out-of-days A term your agent will use when negotiating your shooting schedule on a TV show or movie. Literally, it means how many days you will work out of the total production schedule of days.

day player An actor who hired for one day on a movie or TV show.

dealer spot A national commercial produced and paid for by a national advertiser and then turned over to local dealers to book air time, usually with the dealer's tag added on.

digital video A new technology for capturing visual images. Images are immediately converted to binary code and can be imported into computers, where they can be manipulated and edited.

dolly When the camera moves in toward you or away from you during a shot, that's called dollying. This is different from "zooming," where the camera stays in one place and the lens is shifted for a close-up shot.

downgrade When they hire you as a principal performer in a commercial and for one reason or another your footage winds up on the cutting room floor, they will downgrade you from a principal to an extra. No residuals. It shouldn't happen to your worst enemy.

download When you retrieve a file from the Internet, placing it on your own computer, that's called downloading.

downstage The area in front of the actor when standing on the stage facing the audience.

ECU Abbreviation for extreme close-up. Refers to a tight shot of something; typically seen in film, TV, and commercial scripts.

e-mail The way people in the twenty-first century communicate with one another computer-to-computer.

Equity See **Actors' Equity Association**

Equity principal interview See **open call**

Equity waiver See **waiver**

EXT Abbreviation for exterior; a scene that is shot outside.

first-run syndication Television programs that are produced for and sold to independent TV stations all across the country; this is an alternative to selling a show to one of the three networks, which would, in turn, feed the programming to their affiliates.

foley The enhancement of individual sound effects on film. The sound of footsteps on loose gravel, for example, might be enhanced to sound more ominous. Richard Gere and Debra

Winger's kissing scenes in *An Officer and a Gentleman* were enhanced this way, a fact I can never seem to forget when I watch the movie. The people who do this work are specialists known as foley artists.

franchise An agent signed up with the unions is franchised, that is, approved to represent union talent.

gaffer The chief electrician on a film set.

golden time On a TV or movie set, overtime after the sixteenth hour. It is golden because your pay starts skyrocketing.

half-hour Your call time in the theater. Literally, it means you should be there half an hour before the curtain goes up.

headshot Another name for an 8x10 glossy photo. Don't get this confused with a **composite** or a **Zed card.**

hit On the Internet , when a person visits a web site, that's known as a hit. People are proud when they get a lot of hits on their web sites.

honey wagon Dressing rooms on wheels. You get assigned one of your own when you are working on a TV show or movie. They're called honey wagons because the accompanying toilets can be aromatic. You think I'm pulling your leg, don't you?

IATSE International Alliance of Theatrical Stage Employees and Motion Picture Machine Operators of the United States and Canada. This is one of the two unions that represent editors, camera operators, electricians, set designers, and other crafts on movies and TV shows. The other is **NABET.** It is said that IATSE people may be a little better qualified, but the union is stodgy and given to cronyism.

industrials Also known as corporate films, these are made by businesses for use in training or motivating their employees. There is also such an animal as a live industrial show, where a company stages a Las Vegas– or Broadway-style sales extravaganza, complete with singers and dancers.

INT Abbreviation for interior; a scene shot inside as opposed to outside.

interactive video A film that allows the viewer to interact with what is happening on the screen. It is the product of a marriage between the video disc and the personal computer.

key grip The person on a film set who helps set up the camera, as well as the dolly it sits on.

League of American Theatres and Producers The national association of theatrical producers and theater operators.

location When you are not shooting on a sound stage, you "go on location."

log on When you tell your computer to dial up the Internet, that's logging on. It is necessary to have a modem if you want to log on.

loop Also known as ADR (Automatic Dialogue Replacement), this is what you do when you go into a recording studio, watch film (usually of yourself), and simultaneously record dialogue so that it is in sync with the moving lips up on the screen. Sometimes this is necessary because the sound may have been improperly recorded during filming. Perhaps there was unwanted background noise, so they make a clean sound track and "loop" the dialogue.

LORT Acronym for League of Resident Theatres, a national organization of not-for-profit theaters. Equity has a LORT contract.

manager A person who contractually "manages" a performer's overall career. The usual fee for this service is 15 percent of what you earn. Not to be confused with **agent.**

mark The spot, usually indicated with a piece of tape on the ground, where the actor is supposed to stand when "action" is called. As in "Could you stand on your mark, Roberta?"

M.O.S. An abbreviation for "mit out sound" (without sound). This means they are recording picture but no sound. The origin of the term goes back to the early days of Hollywood when there were a lot of German movie directors who couldn't speak English well. Some say Lothar Mendes was the one to coin it, others say Eric Von Stroheim. Whoever it was, it stuck as an industry term. You'll see it written on the slate.

NABET National Association of Broadcast Employees and Technicians. One of the two unions that represent camera operators and other crafts on movies and TV shows. The other is **IATSE.**

NATPE Acronym for National Association of Television Program Executives. The annual NATPE conference is where producers of shows intended for **first-run syndication** display their wares to buyers from TV stations across the country.

NATR The National Association of Talent Representatives (New York only).

non-Equity A non-Equity stage production is one that may not employ union members. There is pay involved, but it generally will not come up to union minimums, and you won't encounter such niceties as pension and welfare contributions. Don't confuse non-Equity shows with **Equity waiver.**

no quote A term used in TV to indicate that you are receiving less than your usual rate, or "quote," for an acting job, but everybody promises not to tell.

O/C Abbreviation for On Camera. Refers to whatever the camera is seeing, whether a person, place, or thing.

online When you are logged onto the Internet and are surfing around, you are online.

open call Known more formally as an **Equity principal interview,** or on the street as a **cattle call,** this is where the casting process is theoretically thrown open to all comers. You get to hand your picture to a representative of the production, who makes a decision about whether you should get a subsequent audition. People actually get auditions and jobs from these affairs, and in New York they are a way of life.

P.A. Abbreviation for Production Assistant. A fancy word for a gofer.

pan A camera shot that sweeps from side to side. As in "We'll pan with you when you drive by on your bike, Bob."

per diem When you work on location this fee is paid by the producer to compensate for the cost of meals not provided by the producer. In other words, if you have to eat in restaurants, they pay for it.

pickup When a take gets botched while filming, you might do a "pickup," starting in the middle of the scene. It has nothing whatsoever to do with singles bars.

post-production Everything that takes place on a TV show, movie, or commercial after shooting is completed. Editing, for example, is a post-production activity.

prescreen The process whereby a casting director may check you out before you read for the producer and director. It might involve a cold reading, the opportunity to present prepared monologues, or just a meeting.

prime time Network programming aired 8 to 11 P.M. (7 to 10 P.M. in Central/Mountain time zones).

production house The ad agency subcontracts the actual production of a commercial to a production house. Usually a director comes attached to a production house.

quote Your rate; how much you get paid for TV and film.

reel A videotape composite of excerpts from your film, TV, or commercial work. Some actors have several different reels, one for film and TV, another for corporate/industrial, and yet another for commercials. You use them as an extension of your headshot and composite. It is just another way to let potential employers see your work. Also, your mom will like it.

reverse Moving the camera around to shoot the other actor's POV. As in "Okay, Roberta, let's get a reverse on that."

SAG Acronym for Screen Actors Guild, the largest of the performers' unions. Its jurisdiction includes motion pictures and most TV shows, specifically those that are filmed rather than videotaped. SAG also covers many corporate films.

scan Internet term. If you want to put your headshot on your web site, you have to scan it. It is sort of like faxing your photo into cyberspace, and you need a scanner in order to do it. They're not expensive.

search engine The Internet equivalent of the Yellow Pages. Yahoo is the largest search engine.

SEG Acronym for Screen Extras Guild, which used to be one of the affiliated performers' unions but merged with Screen Actors Guild in 1992. There is no more SEG.

set Where performers do their work. As in "When you get out of makeup, I'll take you to the set, Bob."

setup When they move the camera, lights, and the like from the kitchen set to the bathroom set, that change involves a new setup; term used in film.

SFX Abbreviation for sound effects. Refers to things like the sound of a door closing, the sound of coffee being poured, the sound of a distant drum, and so forth.

sides Pages from a movie or TV script that have been excerpted for the purpose of auditions.

signator A producer who has signed an agreement with a union, thereby enabling him or her to employ union talent.

slate In commercial casting, to look in the lens of the camera and say who you are, as in "Slate your name, please." Also, a slate is a device used to indicate which scene and shot is being recorded. Most often, it looks like a little chalkboard, and they take a picture of it just before calling "action!" Sometimes referred to as "sticks."

slug On your 8x10 glossy, the addition of your name. Sometimes called a name slug.

software Once you own a computer, you have to install software on it if you want it to do anything. I wrote this book on the word-processing software called Microsoft Word.

sound stage Literally, a soundproof building used for shooting movies, TV shows, or commercials.

spike In the legitimate theater, fluorescent tape put on the lips of steps and other protrusions so you can see where you are going in the dark.

stage left The actor's left when standing on the stage facing the audience. Note that this is precisely backward from **camera left.**

stage manager The director's right-hand person in the theater, also in charge of running the show once it opens.

stage right The actor's right when standing on the stage facing the audience.

Station 12 The department at SAG that handles cast clearance, such as when you are hired to do a commercial and the casting director checks with SAG to be sure you are eligible to work. If you aren't up to date with your dues, for example, Station 12 will know about it and tell the casting director.

story board A cartoon depiction of what the commercial or movie is going to look like on a shot-by-shot basis. Looks a lot like a black-and-white version of the Sunday comics.

surfing When you go on to the Internet and move from one web site to another, that's surfing. It's like riding a cyberwave.

Taft–Hartley Act An act of Congress specifying that, if an employer has a union shop and wants to hire a nonunion person, then the union is obligated to allow that person to join. It is through the provisions of this act that most people get into SAG, AFTRA, and AEA.

take The period of time the camera is actually rolling, the time between "Action!" and "Cut!" As in "Let's get this in one take, Roberta."

TelePrompter A device in which the script is typed on a long roll of paper and then slowly scrolled during performance for the performer's reference. Used on newscasts, some talk shows, soap operas, and some corporate films. You don't see these on a movie set or in auditions.

test commercial One that is made to run in a very limited market, usually one city. If the product sells there, the spot might be "rolled out" to a broader market.

three bells On a sound stage, three loud, prolonged rings of a bell means a scene is about to be shot, and everybody should be quiet. One loud ring means you can talk again.

top-of-the-show A common term in the TV industry, indicating an unofficial but firm salary ceiling, beyond which the producers theoretically will not negotiate. If you're cast on a sitcom in a guest star role, you will likely be paid "top-of-the-show," probably no more than $1,600 for the episode. Your agent would be unable to negotiate above that.

track Literally, metal tracks laid down so the camera can dolly smoothly. As in "We'll track along with you as you walk to the car, Bob."

traffic department If you want to know where your commercial is running so your mom can see it, call the ad agency and ask for the Traffic Department. They purchase air time and keep up with this kind of thing. Nice folks.

turnaround 1. The number of hours between dismissal one day and call time the next day. 2. A movie studio term used when development of a script is halted. The project is put into turnaround, going back to the producer who brought it in the first place.

TV Q Abbreviation for TV quotient. A controversial survey of the recognizability and liability of TV performers, conducted by Market Evaluation, Inc., in Port Washington, New York. It is said that the results of this survey can dramatically affect a performer's career on TV.

two-shot Two people on camera instead of one (which would, of course, be a "single"). As in "Okay, Roberta, let's get a two-shot."

under five An actor hired to speak fewer than five lines. You hear this term a lot in the world of soap operas. Literally it equates to no more than fifty words. Talk more than that and you get paid more.

upstage The area behind actor when standing on the stage facing the audience. When someone is said to "upstage" you, it actually means he or she is doing something behind your back while you are facing the audience.

URL On the Internet, the Uniform Resource Locator, otherwise known as a web site address. My URL is www.edhooks.com.

waiver In a nutshell, one of the unions is allowing its members to work in a particular production without being paid. Wages are waived. Equity waiver is the term used for stage, and SAG waiver normally applies to certain student films, like those made at American Film Institute, NYU, or USC. The important thing to remember about waiver is that each individual production must be approved by the union. If you are nonunion, you definitely can appear in a waiver show, right alongside union members who are waiving their pay. Not to be confused with nonunion or **non-Equity** situations, where no union approval or involvement is indicated.

walla Crowd sounds in movies and TV shows. It is recorded in the same manner as looping.

Web On the Internet, the World Wide Web, or www for short.

WGA Writers Guild of America. The union for screenwriters.

wildspot When a commercial runs in specific cities instead of on a national basis. The advertiser pays a set fee per city for thirteen weeks of unlimited use. It is possible, even probable, that a spot will run both network and wildspot at the same time.

wrap Finishing a production. "It's a wrap!" Sometimes this is followed by a party.

Zed card A slick, frequently full-color photo card used by professional models. Actors have no need for these at all.

Index

About the Author

Ed Hooks has been acting in theater, film, and television for thirty years. His credits include more than a hundred stage plays in New York, Los Angeles, and regional theaters; TV shows such as *Murder, She Wrote, Full House, Hart to Hart,* and *Home Improvement;* plus numerous films and made-for-TV movies. He has also appeared in TV commercials for more than 150 accounts, including AT&T, Magnavox, Pampers, and McDonald's.

Mr. Hooks, the author of *The Ultimate Scene and Monologue Sourcebook* and *Acting for Animators,* is a highly respected acting teacher. His students, many of whom work prominently in the entertainment industry, number into the thousands. He lives in Palo Alto, California, with his wife and daughter. His e-mail address is edhooks@best.com, and his web site can be found at www.ed hooks.com.